MYTH, LEGEND AND
FOLKLORE SERIES

*British Dragons*

The Dragon of Wantley, killed by More of More Hall

# BRITISH DRAGONS

Jacqueline Simpson

**WORDSWORTH EDITIONS**
*in association with*
**THE FOLKLORE SOCIETY**

FL<sub></sub>S
books

First published in 1980 by B. T. Batsford Limited
4 Fitzhardinge Street, London W1H 0AH
This edition published 2001 by Wordsworth Editions Limited
Cumberland House, Crib Street, Ware, Hertfordshire SG12 9ET
in association with FLS Books, The Folklore Society,
c/o The Warburg Institute, Woburn Square, London WC1H 0AB

Editor FLS Books: Jennifer Chandler

ISBN 1 84022 507 6

Typeset by Antony Gray
Printed and bound in Great Britain by
Mackays of Chatham plc, Chatham, Kent

This exciting new series is made possible by a unique partnership between Wordsworth Editions and The Folklore Society.

Among the major assets of The Folklore Society is its unparalleled collection of books, in the making since 1878. The library and archives have, over the years, formed an invaluable specialist resource. Now, Wordsworth Editions, which is committed to opening up whole areas of culture through good-looking, good-value books and intelligent commentary, make these riches widely available.

Individual introductions by acknowledged experts place each work in historical context and provide commentaries from the perspective of modern scholarship.

PROFESSOR W. F. H. NICOLAISEN
*President, The Folklore Society*

# The Folklore Society

**What is folklore?**   Folklore has been defined as 'traditional culture', but no one phrase can do justice to the subject. It embraces music, song, dance, drama, narrative, language, foods, medicine, arts and crafts, religion, magic and belief. Folklore is the way that people fill their lives with meaning, through the stories they share, the daily rituals they perform. Folklore can be both the expression of our individuality and the source of a sense of community. From standing stones to biker gangs, from ancient riddles to the latest joke craze, from King Arthur to the playground, from birth to death, folklore is the stuff of life.

**The Folklore Society: who we are.**   Since 1878 The Folklore Society has provided a meeting-ground for both academics and enthusiasts eager to learn about popular culture and traditional life. The Society promotes awareness of folklore within universities, museums, festivals, in fact wherever traditional culture is discussed and researched.

The Society has an elected committee which aims to be responsive to its members' needs. It therefore embraces a number of specialist groups, such as the East Anglia Folklore Group, to make the Society accessible to all.

**The Folklore Society: what we do.**   In order to encourage awareness of folklore the Society organises events, prizes and research projects. It runs at least one conference a year, and hosts the annual Katharine Briggs memorial lecture.

The Society publishes its own academic journal, *Folklore*, in association with Routledge. It also produces numerous monographs and pamphlets, either under its own imprint, *FLS Books*, or in conjunction with other publishers.

In addition to the journal *Folklore*, members receive a regular newsletter, *FLS News*, through which they can call on the expertise of the entire Society. They also have access to a specialist library with both reference and lending facilities and a substantial archive. The library constitutes a unique resource for the study of folklore, old and new.

**The Folklore Society: how to contact us.**   For details about how to join The Folklore Society and about our forthcoming activities and publications, contact: The Folklore Society, University College London, Gower Street, London WC1E 6BT

Telephone: 020 7862 8564 (with voice mail)
E-mail: folklore.society@talk21.com
Website: www.folklore–society.com

The Folklore Society is a Registered Charity No.1074552

# Contents

# Introduction

Towards the end of the seventeenth century, when changing ideas in science and religion were playing havoc with traditional beliefs, the antiquarian John Aubrey jotted down a cynical piece of anonymous verse which had caught his fancy:

> To save a maid, St George a dragon slew;
> A pretty tale, if all that's told be true.
> Most say there are no dragons; and 'tis said
> There was no George. Pray God there was a maid!

'Most say there are no dragons' – but this has never stopped poets, artists, storytellers and musicians from exploiting the fascination these mythical beasts exert on the human imagination. In English literature alone we can read of them in *Beowulf*, in various medieval romances of chivalry, in the legend of England's national saint, in Spenser's *Faerie Queene*, in William Morris's epic *Sigurd the Volsung*, and in imaginative fiction by Kenneth Grahame, J. R. R. Tolkien, and many others. In art, a whole book could be written on dragons in sculpture, wood-carvings, manuscript illuminations, heraldry, paintings, stained glass, and book illustrations. And though English opera cannot match the serious dragons in *The Magic Flute* and *Siegfried*, we do have what was once an extremely popular burlesque opera based on a Yorkshire legend, Henry Carey's *The Dragon of Wantley* (1737).

This book will not investigate the dragon as a theme in the history of literature and art; still less will it attempt a psychological interpretation of the subconscious significance of dragons. (This aspect has recently been discussed by Francis Huxley in *The Dragon: Nature of Spirit, Spirit of Nature* 1979.) Its aim is simply to gather and examine the material to be found in localised folktales in England, Scotland and Wales, together with certain folk customs in which dragon-images were used; the general history of dragons is confined to the first chapter, as a necessary background to understanding our own traditional stories. In the same way, comparative material from the rest of Europe is only briefly and occasionally mentioned.

The British material is remarkably extensive. Over seventy villages and small towns (listed in Appendix B) still have a tradition about a local dragon, or can be shown on good evidence to have had such a tradition in the past; since in several cases the legend exists in two or three variants differing in some significant detail of plot, there are actually about 80 stories to be considered. Very likely, there are still more examples that have escaped my notice, and I would be grateful to readers who might tell me of them.

The book opens with a survey of the background; after assessing the hypothesis of a link between prehistoric reptiles and the origins of the concept of dragons, it traces in outline the history of Occidental dragons from their first appearance in early cosmic myths through to the period when naturalists abandoned belief in their existence as real animals. Then in Chapters 2, 3 and 4, I discuss British local dragon legends from three different angles: how they describe the appearance, size, habits and habitats of the dragons; what types of person are chosen as heroes; and what methods are described for overcoming the monsters. This analysis reveals a variety of curious points; for instance, a recurrent link between dragons and watery environment, the influence of various beliefs popularly held about serpents, a frequent link with the prestige of local landowning families, and a very marked taste for grotesque humour and ingenious trickery in the methods of despatching dragons. It also overthrows many expectations one might have from reading other types of dragon-slaying tales such as those in Germanic legends, saints' lives, or fairytales; for example, the dragon of local legend does not live in wild, remote areas; it is not normally associated with spiritual evil; the hero never brings back treasures from its lair; and in only one case is there a princess to be rescued.

Chapter 5 examines the way in which the legends are integrally related to their topographical settings, and the vital role played by material objects including tombstones, paintings, heraldic devices and landscape features, both as stimuli to the formation of legends and as 'proofs' of their veracity. Chapter 6 deals with the dragon effigies made for use in processions, pageants, and medieval plays. One town, Norwich, still owns two of these effigies whose predecessors can be traced back for over 550 years; another, Chester, has preserved vivid documentary accounts of dragons in pageants of the sixteenth and seventeenth centuries. Other evidence also tends to show that such monster-figures were once a popular feature in various forms of merrymaking, evoking both amusement and affection. Finally, Chapter 7 draws upon the evidence assembled in the previous chapters to answer, as far as possible, certain general questions: What support, if any, can be found in local legends for the various hypotheses commonly put forward to explain the origins of dragon stories? What sociological and psychological functions do they fulfil that could account for their wide distribution, their continued survival, and their popularity? What points do they convey, and what pleasures do they give? The conclusion reached, briefly, is that these stories do not owe their popularity to any religious, mythological or politico-historical symbolism, but to their value in fostering a proud sense of communal identity (sometimes linked with the prestige of certain families); they also offer the aesthetic pleasures of exciting narrative that is full of a sense of drama, and often enlivened with humour, ingenuity, and an element of surprise.

These traditional tales, we can safely assume, were in oral circulation for generations before they were put into print in greater or lesser detail, and sometimes with a consciously literary rehandling, either by specialist collectors of folklore or, more often, by local writers simply interested in the history and legends of their own districts. Most of these printed versions belong to the nineteenth and twentieth centuries, but there are also a fair number of earlier allusions (generally brief) which enable us to trace certain dragon legends back to the seventeenth, sixteenth, or even the fifteenth centuries (see Appendix C). In many cases, the tales are still well known in their localities, being kept alive partly through printed media (such as guidebooks), but partly also by word of mouth. The sources I have used can be identified through the Notes and Bibliography; several of the best ones, to which frequent references are made, are reprinted in full in Appendix A.

My chief debt of gratitude is to the Folklore Society, without whose library this dragon hunt would scarcely have been possible. I am also grateful to Dr E. C. Cawte, Mrs Ellen Ettlinger, Dr K. P. Oakley, Miss Christina Hole, Mrs Doris Jones-Baker, Mr Alan Smith, Mr J. Main of Durham County Library and Mr Richard Lane for helpful conversations and correspondence.

And now, in the words of the traditional song *The Lambton Worm*:

> Whisht, lads, and hold your gobs,
> And I'll tell you all an awful story;
> Whisht, lads, and hold your gobs,
> And I'll tell you about the Worm.

# A Note on the Second Edition

In the twenty years since this book was first published in 1980, not much new material has come my way; what little there is strengthens the links between dragon legends, local gentry and their armorial devices, and local topography that I found to be typical of the genre.

The only completely fresh story that has been brought to my notice is located at Hughenden, near High Wycombe, Buckinghamshire; I am grateful to Clive Harper for sending me his pamphlet 'The Hughenden Dragon' (Torsdag Publications, 1985). The earliest mention of this tale was in a letter from Edgar Bochart in *The Gentleman's Magazine* of October 1758, pp. 466–7. A woman was repeatedly alarmed by seeing a large water serpent in a pond where she drew water, but agreed to sit beside the pond to attract it to herself, so that the villagers could ambush and kill it; this plan worked, and the snake's stuffed skin was displayed at a nearby farm till it rotted, and then replaced by a dragon-like painting, which Bochart was shown. This farm was the old manor house of Rockalls, near Hughenden Church; both manor and church had heraldic carvings showing the arms of the Wellesbourne family, which include a griffin (easily confused with a dragon) holding a child in one claw. Mr Harper kindly informs me that after he published his pamphlet an old lady told him that when she was a child her father warned her to keep away from the pond because a dragon there had once swallowed a baby in a pram, and the woman pushing the pram.

Glyn Morgan's *Secret Essex* (1982), pp. 73–5, gives a fuller version of the Hornden story than I do in Ch. 7. It seems that Sir James Tyrell fell dead on reaching home after slaying the snake; his son then went to see the monster's carcass and tripped over it, breaking his leg, which became gangrenous and caused him to die too. This final episode I would regard as influenced by legends of the 'fated death' type, such as the one from Anglesea I mention on p. 71.

I am grateful to Mr N. A. Hudleston for informing me that Arthur St Clair Brooke's *Slingsby and its Castle* (1904) gives a more detailed topographical account of the habitat of the Slingsby dragon, and that here, too, there is a heraldic link, since the Wyville family have a wyvern in their coat of arms. Also to Mr J. I. Dent, who pointed out an error in the document used by William Camden in his account of Sir Hugh Bardolfe's fight with the dragon at Castle Carlton: there is no place called 'Wormesgay' in Lincolnshire, but the Bardolfes did hold the manor of Wormgay or Wormegay in Norfolk. Mr Dent also kindly told me about carvings of St George and the Dragon on the Ethelbert Gate of Norwich Cathedral, modern replacements for worn originals of *c*.1300; these may well have been the earliest representation of this saint's story in England, predating the upsurge in his cult associated with Edward III (see pp. 105).

An article by David Hey in *Rural History: Economy, Society, Culture* 4:1 (1993), pp. 23–40, investigates the ballad of 'The Dragon of Wantley'; he argues that the 'dragon' was not Sir Francis Wortley, as Bishop Percy was told (see pp. 130–1), but his father, Sir Richard Wortley (d. 1603), who was involved in bitter disputes over hunting rights and over tithes. He also notes that the Mores had a dragon as the crest of their arms in 1634, possibly indicating a version of the story predating the publication of the ballad in 1685.

Ralph Whitlock's *Here Be Dragons* was published in 1983; it covers many of the same legends as the present work, sometimes giving additional or variant information that supplements my own – for example, that at Sockburn an ancient gravestone showing a man with an axe confronting snaky monsters is held to 'confirm' the local legend: while the church at Saffron Walden used to display the sword which slew the cockatrice, plus an effigy of the creature itself, until these objects were destroyed in the Civil War.

*October 2000*

# Acknowledgement

The author and publishers would like to thank Janet and Colin Bord for their kind permission to reproduce the illustrations used in this book – the Dragon of Wantley on page 2; the dragon from Edward Topsell's *The Historie of Serpents* on page 16 and the Lambton Worm from an anonymous pamphlet of 1875 on page 81.

The superscript numerals in the text refer to the Notes at the end of the book

A dragon, as drawn by Edward Topsell in *The Historie of Serpents*, 1608. Like other early naturalists, he may have been misled by man-made fakes

# CHAPTER ONE

# The Background: Dragons down the Ages

In 1608, the naturalist Edward Topsell wrote the following in his book *The Historie of Serpents*:

> Among all the kindes of Serpentes, there is none comparable to the Dragon, or that affordeth and yeeldeth so much plentifull matter in historie for the ample discovery of the nature thereof; and therefore heerein I must borrow more time . . . than peradventure the Reader would be willing to spare . . . But I will strive to make the description pleasant, with variable history, seeing I may not avoid the lengthe heereof.

A folklorist can heartily endorse these words, though from a different standpoint, since even though it is now impossible to maintain as Topsell did that the dragon is or ever was a real animal, one serpent among other serpents, it remains true that the traditional belief in his existence 'yeeldeth much plentifull matter' which extends widely in time and space. Tales, beliefs, and artistic representations concerning dragons can be found in many different lands, both Western and Oriental, and can even be traced in the two earliest recorded mythologies, the Babylonian and the Indian. Furthermore, both the characteristics of the creatures and the attitudes of storytellers towards them have varied in truly protean fashion, so that one can find dragons of earth, water or sky; destructive dragons and benevolent dragons; dragons of cosmic myth and dragons of comic anecdote; dragons as symbols of evil and dragons as emblems of national or family honour; dragons as treasure-guardians, as man-eaters, as luck-bringers, as portents of disaster, as bringers of rain, as bringers of drought, as bestowers of magical wisdom, or simply as monsters whose sole function is to be killed off by a hero. Broadly speaking, the major contrast is between the traditions of Europe and the Near East, where the dragon is predominantly regarded as a dangerous, destructive, and even morally evil creature, and those of the Far East, where he is almost always seen as benevolent and protective, and a stern enforcer of moral justice. To consider the rich Oriental lore is beyond the scope of this book; one may, however, pause to note that the noble and auspicious Chinese dragon, the Lung, is now a familiar sight in Western cities that have Chinese communities; for instance, its image could be seen dancing through the centre of London in the summer of 1977, as the Chinese of Soho celebrated the Queen's silver jubilee.

Before considering British traditions in detail, it is necessary to attempt some survey, however sketchy, of the main lines of development in the evolution of European dragon lore, and to consider that inevitable but probably unanswerable question: how did mankind begin to believe in dragons? And indeed, even more basically, what is it that men through the ages have meant by various words we conventionally translate as 'dragon'?

The word 'dragon' is derived, through Latin *draco*, from the Greek *drakon*, which refers to any large snake, whether in real life or in a mythological setting. When 'dragon' is chosen by Europeans to translate a term for a monster in some other language, such as Hebrew, Babylonian, Hindi or Chinese, the choice implies that the monster is of basically reptilian type. Obviously, many cultures describe their dragons as having secondary features drawn from different species of animals, particularly wings, claws and manes; with water-dwelling dragons it can sometimes be hard to draw a dividing line between reptilian types and monstrous fish. Nevertheless, it is the reptilian traits that predominate, whether these are based on the crocodile, the lizard, or (most often) the snake. In many cases, the monster is said to be immensely large, far beyond the dimensions of any living reptile.

## The Role of Prehistoric Animals

Time and again in the last one hundred and fifty years or so, as scientific discoveries revealed the extraordinary fossils of prehistoric animals, students of mythology have proposed the romantic theory that the concept of the dragon is a 'racial memory' of the large carnivorous dinosaurs of prehistoric ages. This notion was excusable in the early decades of palaeontology, when the geological timescale was not clearly understood (at any rate by the general public), and when 'gaps' between species and eras were constantly being 'closed' by fresh discoveries of hitherto unknown forms of life. It therefore did not at first seem too implausible to suggest that dinosaurs survived long enough, or man developed early enough, for the two species to have encountered each other. By the end of the nineteenth century, however, this idea was rejected as totally impossible not only by biologists and palaeontologists but by folklorists as well; as E. S. Hartland wrote in *The Legend of Perseus* (1896):

The suggestion has often been made that these stories are traditions of the saurians which abounded in geological times. Of this, not a particle of evidence has been adduced; and it is in itself so wildly improbable as barely to deserve notice. None of the giant reptiles of the secondary period were contemporary with man. The process of evolution was still far short of that consummation. And when man appeared in the Quaternary, or perhaps at an advanced stage of the Tertiary period, the remains of iguanodons and pterodactyls had long been peacefully fossilized beyond his reach.[1]

The revisions of the evolutionary timescale since Hartland wrote have only served to accentuate the impossibility. Admittedly, the earliest types of man are now regarded as between one and two million years old, but even so there is a gap of not less than sixty or seventy million years between the extinction of the dinosaurs and the evolution of the first men. It has therefore been proposed by those who cling tenaciously to the equation between dragon and dinosaur that the 'racial memory' was inherited by man from his remote non-human ancestors, the primitive mammals which were contemporary with the great reptiles. These early ancestors of ours were still a very long way from being monkeys, let alone hominids; they were, at that time, small squirrel-like insect-eating creatures, very similar to the present-day Asiatic tree-shrew in size, habits and brain capacity. No doubt they were terrified of even the smallest dinosaur, but to think that we can 'remember' their experiences of sixty million years ago is wilder than the wildest myth.

But, it may be said, is it quite certain that all dinosaurs really are extinct? Was not the coelacanth, an archaic type of fish that flourished during the Devonian Period three hundred million years ago, caught alive in the seas off Africa in 1938 and again in 1952? May there not be other unsuspected survivals in the depths of the oceans, for instance some of the large swimming reptiles, the plesiosaurs? This of course raises the fascinating and controversial problem of the Sea Serpent and his freshwater cousin, the Loch Ness Monster. There have been innumerable theories to account for these, either as observations of known animals such as giant squids, eels, swimming pythons, or the oarfish (which is a curiously snake-like fish with spikes down its back), or as glimpses of hitherto unknown species such as long-necked seals or gigantic newts or worms. Among all the theories, that of a surviving plesiosaur remains highly popular among the general public; if such a creature did exist, it could easily account not only for Nessie and the Sea Serpent, but also for the many water-dwelling dragons in the local legends of various countries. But one must admit that if it does exist it has been remarkably discreet about its funerals, for sixty million years it has contrived to dispose of its dead so neatly that not a bone, not a claw, not a scale or a tooth has ever been brought to light. Maybe, in view of the coelacanth, such a state of affairs is not totally impossible, but until material evidence comes to light it must remain, in Hartland's words, 'wildly improbable'.

But Hartland was certainly wrong when he wrote that the remains of the extinct dinosaurs were 'peacefully fossilized beyond [man's] reach'. Fossils are by no means out of reach; they can be exposed by erosion, by floods and landslips, be found in caves, or be unearthed during mining operations, and presumably in earlier periods they must have been found much more readily than today, simply lying about in remote areas where men rarely went. There are plenty of recorded incidents in Europe in comparatively recent times where large fossil bones of extinct animals (for instance, mammoths and woolly rhinoceros) were assumed to be bones of giants or of dragons; until the last few years it was possible to buy various kinds of fossils in China under the general term of 'dragons' bones'.

There are at least two cases where it can be shown that a knowledge of fossils influenced the way in which dragons were represented in art. One is a relief showing a four-legged dragon in the church at Rentweisdorf in Coburg, where the artist has clearly been influenced by having seen a fossilised plesiosaur; it has been suggested that skeletons of these creatures became well known in the later Middle Ages when liass slate was being mined on a large scale in Swabia, liass being a type of rock rich in their fossils. The second case concerns the statue which stands in the marketplace at Klagenfuhrt in Austria, and which was erected there in the latter part of the sixteenth century, of a giant killing a dragon. The dragon here has a most unusual head, copied from the skull of a woolly rhinoceros which had been unearthed in the district in 1355; until recently, the skull itself was preserved in Klagenfuhrt Town Hall.[2]

Bones are not the only type of fossil. In certain circumstances, footprints in mud or sand can become fossilised, and then may reappear to startle observers millions of years later. On 28 January 1978, *The Times* reported, with photograph:

> Winter storms have uncovered footprints measuring about two feet across on soft mudstone at Bexhill-on-Sea, East Sussex. They are believed to have been made by a species of prehistoric dinosaur, probably an iguanodon, which lived when Bexhill enjoyed a subtropical climate more than a hundred million years ago. Mr Henry Sargent, curator of Bexhill Museum, said the prints would have been made on marshy, freshwater ground. What is now the seashore was probably at that time the edge of a swamp or lake. The prints were found by Mr

Frederick Cornford, a Rother District Council Worker, during a routine inspection of sea defences.

Had anybody found tracks like these during any period before our present scientific age, he could have drawn only one conclusion from the evidence of his own eyes: some huge three-toed creature, larger than any known animal, had emerged from the sea and walked along the shore. It is through such incidents that long-dead dinosaurs (and other extinct animals, not necessarily reptilian) certainly helped to reinforce the dragon myth.

Contemporary animals helped too, especially if dead and decomposing. Another recent issue of *The Times*, 21 July 1977, carried the report:

> Japanese fishermen caught a dead monster, weighing two tons and thirty feet in length, off the coast of New Zealand in April, it was reported today. Believed to be a survivor of a prehistoric species, the monster was caught at a depth of a thousand feet off the South Island coast, near Christchurch. Palaeontologists from the Natural Science Museum near Tokyo have concluded that the beast belonged to the plesiosaurus family – huge, small-headed reptiles with a long neck and four fins . . . After a member of the crew had photographed and measured it, the trawler''s captain ordered the corpse to be thrown back into the sea for fear of contamination to his fish.

Unfortunately, this fascinating news item led nowhere; no further information appeared in *The Times*, but a BBC bulletin on 30 July announced that the analysis of some tissues which the captain had kept had shown proteins typical of the flesh of the blue shark, a fish that can reach 40 feet in length. The alleged plesiosaur, the potential Sea Serpent, was only a badly decomposed shark.

So, too, was a carcass found on the rocks of Stronsay in the Orkneys in September 1808, which caused great excitement. Various fragments of it, including the skull, were taken to Edinburgh where a prominent naturalist, Dr John Barclay, declared them to be the remains of an unknown animal which he reconstructed as a long, thin, lizard-like creature with three pairs of legs and a spiny ridge down its back, distinctly dragonish in appearance. Most of the fragments were then thrown away, but luckily two vertebrae had been preserved by one of the original witnesses on Stronsay. These were submitted to Sir Everard Home, a leading London ichthyologist, who easily identified them as bones of a large basking shark.[3]

Forty years later something similar happened in Northumberland, though there the identification of the creature was tackled in a more reasonable manner. *The Illustrated London News* of 19 May 1849 reported:

A strange and hitherto unknown fish, nearly thirteen feet in length and possessing many of the characteristics which the captain of the *Daedalus* enumerated in his description of the Great Sea Snake, has really been caught off the Northumbrian coast by the Cullercoats fishermen, and has been exhibited in Newcastle, where it has created the greatest sensation. The Natural History Society of that town have duly reported upon it, and expressed their opinion that it is a young specimen of the genus *Gymnetrus* . . . The present specimen has become the property of a Newcastle merchant, who has presented it to the museum of that town.[4]

A recent American writer upon sea-monsters has suggested that this particular creature is more likely to have been a specimen of the weird-looking snake-like oarfish, *regalecus glesne*, which has more than once been taken for an immature Sea Serpent. Be that as it may, it is clear that carcasses like these must have been found many times in past centuries, and that they, like fossil bones and footprints, and like exaggerated rumours of deadly reptiles in far-off lands, all contributed to the strength and persistence of the dragon legend.

Whether they can be regarded as its actual origin is more doubtful. The human mind seems to have a passion for constructing monsters onto which to project its feelings of awe, terror or aggression, and does not always require confirmatory evidence from the external world in order to believe in the reality of its own creations. There is nothing in nature, for instance, which can possibly be interpreted as evidence for the existence of huge demonic flies, yet such creatures were feared as emissaries of magicians in areas as far apart as Iceland and Sardinia. Probably the roots of all such fantasies lie within the human mind, whose irrational fears and hates find exaggerated expression in the terrifying experiences of dreams, delirium and drugs. Among these mental images, many must remain private to the individual who experiences them. Others, one may suppose, are adopted by a social group and pass into its repertoire of storytelling, art and religious symbolism, after which any further evidence (whether from visionary experiences, from material objects, or from travellers' tales and suchlike rumours) will be judged by reference to the now accepted stereotype, and will serve to reinforce it more and more strongly. In the case of the dragon, however, we can never hope to discover the earliest stages of this process, for they had already occurred before the earliest myths and epics now preserved had been composed. The search for origins, fascinating though its speculations are, is here doomed to failure; instead, there opens up an equally broad field of enquiry – what function has the image of the dragon fulfilled in the various cultures through which it can be traced?

## Early Cosmic Myths

The earliest examples of dragon-like monsters are to be found in the context of cosmological mythology, in the hymns and religious epics of two of the most ancient cultures whose written records have come down to us. One is the Hindu *Ṛg Veda*, in which one hymn in honour of Indra celebrates his slaying of Vṛtra, a creature of cosmic menace described as a 'shoulderless' being, i.e. one of snake-like form. The second is the Babylonian Epic of Creation, the *Enuma Elish*, in which the god Marduk destroys a cosmic goddess of the waters, Tiamat, who is at war with the gods and has created a host of monsters to attack them. Most, though not all, translators and scholars think that Tiamat's own shape was that of a monstrous serpent, and hence identify her with the dragon that is shown on certain Babylonian cylinder-seals.

Which of these two myths is the older is hard to say. The *Ṛg Veda* is thought to have been written down about 1200 BC, but only after the hymns of which it is composed had been in oral use for many centuries. Similarly, the *Enuma Elish*, generally dated to about 1700 BC, incorporates many earlier traditions going back to about 2000 BC. But precise dating is not needed in the present discussion; it is enough to realise that in the earliest myths that have survived the dragon already plays a prominent role, and that several of his most characteristic features and activities are already fully evolved.

Here then, is the Hindu myth of the combat of Indra and Vṛtra, as told in its oldest version:

> I will tell the heroic deeds of Indra, those which the Wielder of the Thunderbolt first accomplished. He slew the dragon and released the waters; he split open the bellies of the mountain. He slew the dragon who lay upon the mountain; Tvastr fashioned the roaring thunderbolt for him. Like lowing cows, the waters have flowed straight down to the ocean . . . Indra, when you killed the first-born of dragons and over-came the deluding lures of the wily, at that very moment you brought forth the sun, heaven and dawn; since then you have found no overpowering enemy. Indra killed Vṛtra, the greater enemy, the shoulderless one, with his great and deadly thunderbolt. Like the branches of a tree felled by the axe, the dragon lies prostrate upon the ground . . . Without feet or hands he fought against Indra, who struck him on the back with his thunderbolt. The castrated steer who wished to become the equal of the virile bull, Vṛtra lay shattered in many places. Over him, as he lay like a broken reed, the swelling waters flowed for man. Those waters that Vṛtra had enclosed with his might – the dragon now lay at their feet . . . When Indra slew Vṛtra, he split open the outlet of the waters that had been closed . . . [5]

Later, as the vast corpus of Indian mythological writings and epic poems developed, the combat of Indra and Vṛtra underwent various elaborations. For instance, the epic *Mâhabhârata* includes one episode in which Vṛtra seizes Indra in his mouth to swallow him, whereupon the other gods instantly create a God of Yawning whose power forces Vṛtra to open his jaws, so that Indra escapes. The final defeat of Vṛtra here involves trickery. The gods had sworn never to harm him with wood or stone or weapon or missile, neither by day nor by night; but Indra, finding him on the shore at twilight, takes a mass of sea-foam, blends into it the power of his thunderbolt and of the God Vishnu, and thus slays Vṛtra without breaking the literal terms of the oath.

The combat of Marduk against Tiamat in the Babylonian epic has some points of likeness with the Indian myth. Marduk, like Indra, is acting as champion on behalf of all the gods, and he too is armed with a thunderbolt, as well as with a mace, a net, bow and arrows, and a team of seven fierce winds. There is a prolonged battle, till eventually:

> The Evil Wind, which followed behind, he let loose in her face.
> When Tiamat opened her mouth to consume him,
> He drove in the Evil Wind, that she closed not her lips.
> As the fierce winds charged her belly,
> Her body was distended and her mouth wide open.
> He released the arrow, it tore her belly,
> It cut through her insides, splitting the heart.
> Having thus subdued her, he extinguished her life.
> He cast down her carcass to stand upon it.[6]

These myths are not, as might seem at first sight, clear-cut ethical allegories in which morally righteous gods destroy morally wicked monsters. If one tries to 'read' them on the ethical level one finds only confusion, since the destructiveness which makes Vṛtra and Tiamat a threat to the existence of the gods is due to their justified wish to avenge a murder committed by those very gods. Vṛtra, as we learn from the later texts, had been created as an instrument of vengeance by one of the gods, whose son, an ascetic of immense spiritual power, had been killed by Indra's thunderbolt. And Tiamat is herself a goddess (indeed, she is ancestress of all other gods except her husband Apsu), and the fury which turned her into an agent of destruction was aroused when the holy Apsu was slain unjustly by his and Tiamat's descendants.

The issues involved are not ethical, but cosmic; these myths are concerned with the creative process that shaped the universe and restored order after a threat of chaos, or of grave deficiences in the natural order. Thus the death of Vṛtra releases the imprisoned waters which were held back by the coils of his body (a potent image in a land as dependent upon rain as India), and at the same moment the sun, the heavens and the dawn are created, and the cosmic order imperilled by his power is re-established. Similarly, Marduk uses Tiamat's body in an act of world-building which involves the restraint and control of waters (for in Babylonia flood, not drought, was the chief peril), and thus ensures the formation of an ordered universe:

> The Lord trod upon the legs of Tiamat,
> With his unsparing mace he crushed her skull.
> When the arteries of her blood he had severed,
> He split her like a shellfish into two parts.
> Half of her he set up and ceiled it as the sky,
> Pulled down the bar and posted guards,
> He bade them to allow not her waters to escape.

There is an ambivalence in the structure of the universe as perceived by these ancient myth-makers. The message is explicitly stated in Hinduism, which teaches the eternal interdependence of order and chaos, construction and destruction, stable pattern and transforming energy, death and birth. No wonder then that the dragons of these myths are profoundly mysterious beings, not to be lightly categorised as 'good' or 'evil'. The most one can say is that the god who kills them performs a creative act and establishes a world-order that is beneficial to gods and men; in both cases, he also wins the kingship over the other gods by accomplishing this deed.

Allusions to a dragon-slaying also occur in other cultures of the ancient Near East, and in these too it seems to have been a mythical act of great importance. For instance, Egyptian texts refer to the great destruction wrought by Ra or Seth on a serpent named Apep or Apophis, who symbolises darkness; every night Apep attacks the boat of the sun-god and is bound or cut to pieces, yet returns next night to renew the combat. The Ugaritic tablets (of about 1400 BC) show that the Canaanites had a similar myth about Baal, of whom it is said, 'Thou smotest Lotan the slippery serpent, madest an end of the wriggling serpent, the tyrant with seven heads.' 'Lotan' is the same word as 'Leviathan'. The story of Baal's destruction of Lotan must have passed into Hebrew mythology, where it was transferred to Yahweh, and where it is represented as a great creative act closely associated with God's control of the primeval waters. There is a clear allusion to it in Psalm 74:

> Thou didst divide the sea by thy strength;
> Thou breakest the heads of the dragons in the waters.
> Thou breakest the heads of Leviathan in pieces,

> Thou gavest him to be meat to the people inhabiting
>                                              the wilderness.
> Thou didst cleave fountain and flood,
> Thou driest up mighty rivers.

This Hebrew monster is also known as Rahab 'The Defiant', as in Psalm 84 and in Isaiah 51 ('Art thou not it that cut Rahab in pieces, that pierced the dragon? Art thou not it that dried up the sea, the waters of the great deep?'). The Book of Job includes both an allusion to Rahab and a lengthy description of Leviathan, who sounds there more like a mere crocodile than a primeval chaos symbol. In Isaiah 27, the cosmic dragon-fight is transferred from the mythical past to the eschatological future, when, in 'the day of the Lord . . . Yahweh with his sore and great and strong sword shall punish Leviathan the swift serpent, and Leviathan the crooked serpent, and he shall slay the dragon that is in the deep sea.'[7] Such passages already begin to foreshadow the role of the dragon as a symbol of the Devil which later dominates Christian writings and iconography.

## Serpents and Sea-monsters in Classical Myths

Turning to ancient Greece, where the word *drakon* covers snakes of many sorts, both real and fantastic, we find a variety of new themes emerging, as well as old ones persisting. The conflict of sky-god and serpent-monster is still present, in the combat of Zeus and Typhon; and the dragon who prevents access to springs of water is found again as the one Cadmus slew at the Spring of Ares on the site of Thebes. But we now also encounter others that guard treasures, for instance Ladon who was coiled round the tree bearing the golden apples of the Hesperides (Herakles shot him with an arrow), and a 'loathsome and immortal dragon of a thousand coils' which guarded the oak on which the Golden Fleece was hung (Medea put him magically to sleep).

Then there is Python, the huge serpent who possessed the oracular shrine at Delphi until Apollo slew him and made the shrine his own; in local Greek cults there was a widespread link between serpents and the benevolent protective dead, the 'heroes' and ancestors in the Underworld, who in turn were connected with oracular and healing shrines. It is presumed that this association of ideas arose from the observation of two facts: the snake's habit of living underground and vanishing rapidly into holes when disturbed, and its unique ability to shed its skin, which seemed a secret power of ever-renewed youth, a form of immortality. Consequently, live serpents were kept in many oracular and healing shrines, while in art serpents were represented in close association with the ancestral dead, the heroes, and certain divine or semi-divine figures such as Hermes and Aesculapius; they symbolised renewed life, healing, prophecy, secret wisdom, and the beneficent aspects of the Underworld, including its gifts of fertility and prosperity. They were also venerated as the *genius*, the protective, luck-bringing guardian of an individual or a family, in both Greece and Rome; their association with prosperity was so close that there were even some little money-boxes made in the shape of a coiled snake with a coin-slot in its body.[8] In short, in the Classical cultures the *drakon* was in many ways an auspicious, though awe-inspiring, figure, protector of literal or metaphorical riches. Of course, from the point of view of the treasure-stealing hero of an adventure tale, like Jason, a treasure-guarding dragon was an obstacle.

However, heroes in Greek tales are also pitted against a variety of purely destructive monsters, of which the two best-known are the Hydra that Herakles slew with the help of Iolaus, and the sea-beast (*ketos*) that Perseus slew in order to save Andromeda. The Hydra, whose name means 'water-creature', lived in a swamp near the source of a river, had a poisonous breath and smell, and a considerable number of heads (9, 50, or 100) which could replace themselves as fast as they were cut off, until Iolaus thought of cauterising each stump with a burning branch. Another of Herakles's exploits, described by Diodorus Siculus, was a combat with a sea-monster (*ketos*) on the Trojan coast, the creature having been sent by Poseidon to devour the inhabitants and spew salt water over all their crops. The king of Troy had been forced to leave his daughter Hesione chained naked to a rock for the monster to eat, but Herakles released her; he then had a wall built by the sea and hid behind it till the monster drew near with open jaws, whereupon he leaped down its throat, fully armed. For three days he remained inside it, hacking it to pieces from within, and at last emerged victorious, but completely bald. His reward was to have been a pair of immortal horses and also, some say, marriage to Hesione; in the event, he received neither, for the king of Troy cheated him.

The similarity with the tale of Perseus and Andromeda is obvious; in both, a woman is about to be sacrificed, and the hero's courage entitles him to her hand, though her parents later break faith with him. We are here a mere hair's breadth away from the standard plot of an internationally known fairytale, 'The Dragon Slayer', to which the legend of St George is also related; the chief difference is that in the fairytale the hero's last-minute difficulties are not due to the princess's parents but to a treacherous companion or onlooker who tries to steal the credit for the deed.[9] In such tales, the stress is on the hero's courage and the reward it brings him; the dragon itself, however luridly it may be described, no longer has any significance or symbolism beyond that of general destructiveness and danger.

## Judeo-Christian Interpretations

In the world of Judaism and early Christianity things took a very different course. By the first century BC, Hebrew thinkers had developed a theory that the serpent in the Garden of Eden was no mere 'beast of the field', however 'subtle', but was identical with Satan, who by then had assumed considerable importance as a figure symbolising evil. This identification may be due to influence from Persian Zoroastrian teachings, since these include one myth in which Ahriman, the Principle of Evil, takes on the form of a serpent; or it may simply be an elaboration of the ancient myth of the chaos-dragon. Whatever its source, the idea struck deep roots in both Jewish and Christian belief, and had far-reaching effects in literature and art. One key passage, from Genesis, was God's mysterious declaration to the serpent, 'I will put enmity between thee and the woman, and between thy seed and her seed; it shall bruise thy head, and thou shalt bruise his heel.' This was taken as prophesying Christ's victory over Satan, or else (in Roman Catholic translations based on the inaccurate reading '*she* shall bruise thy head') as alluding to the Virgin Mary's triumphant resistance, as Second Eve, to the Devil's power that defeated the first Eve – hence the paintings, statues and medals that show the Virgin trampling on a snake. Even more influential was the description in Revelation 12 of 'the great red dragon having seven heads and ten horns' which tried to devour the newborn child of the 'woman clothed with the sun' (who is, in early interpretations, the Christian Church, and in later ones the Virgin Mary). This dragon is explicitly identified with Satan:

> There was war in Heaven; Michael and his angels fought against the dragon; and the dragon fought, and his angels, and prevailed not, neither was their place found any more in Heaven. And the great dragon was cast out, that old serpent, called the Devil, and Satan, which deceiveth the whole world; he was cast out into the earth, and his angels were cast out with him. And I heard a loud voice saying in Heaven, Now is come salvation, and strength, and the kingdom of our God, and the power of his Christ, for the accuser of our brethren is cast down, which accused them before our God day and night. And they overcame him by the blood of the Lamb . . .

The splendour of this imagery echoes and re-echoes down the Christian centuries, setting up a firm link between Devil and dragon that still rouses an immediate response wherever we encounter it, whether in Russian icons, in the carvings in a medieval church, in Spenser, or in William Dunbar's fine poem, *On the Resurrection of Christ*:

> Done is a batell on the dragon blak,
> Our campioun Chryst confountet has his force . . .

Moreover, the same symbolism was extended to the triumphs of human champions of the true religion. Thus Daniel, in an apocryphal passage which was accepted as an authentic part of the Old Testament until the Reformation, was credited with killing a dragon by tossing a ball of pitch, fat and hair down its throat. In the same way the triumphs of Christian saints over paganism and vice could be represented in terms of a miraculous power over serpents – a literalised application of Christ's symbolic promises to faithful disciples, 'They shall take up serpents, and if they drink any deadly thing, it shall not hurt them' (Mark 16:18), and 'Behold, I give you power to tread on serpents and scorpions, and over all the power of the enemy' (Luke 10:19).

The result, as hagiography and iconography developed during the course of the Middle Ages, was a whole host of stories about saints who curse or banish snakes, turn them into stone or trample them underfoot, drink unharmed from goblets containing poisonous snakes or lizards, and subdue or slaughter dragons. There are said to be over forty dragon-slaying saints in the Western Church alone. They include, besides the famous St George, St Philip the Apostle, St Margaret of Antioch, St Martha, St Florent, St Victor, the Breton saints Samson and Armel (both Welsh by origin), St Hilary of Poitiers, St Clement of Metz, St Romain of Rouen, St Germanus, St Radegunde, and the Irish saints Beircheart and Ciaran, who both drove a dragon into a lake. Some of these were only locally famous, others much more widely known. In these legends, more stress is usually laid on religious procedures than on combat; normally the saint kills or banishes the dragon by simply showing it a crucifix, sprinkling it with holy water, or binding it with a priestly stole – or, in the case of a female saint, with the girdle that symbolises her virginity. The dragons are often said to live in or near water and to prey on beasts and men, but they also sometimes bring plague or breathe fire, as befits emissaries of Hell. In any case, they are most thoroughly and unambiguously evil – at least, when described in the official Saint's Life, though local attitudes as reflected in folk festivals are very different, as will be seen in Chapter 6.

## Emblems of Valour

With all this load of symbolism upon his back, the dragon might well have become, by the end of the Middle Ages, the world's most hated imaginary denizen. However, a counter-current had been flowing since the time of the Roman Empire which tended to establish him as an emblem of national valour. In Rome, the ferocious aspects of dragons appealed to soldiers in search of warlike insignia; they were used as emblems for cohorts, just as eagles were for legions. It is recorded that at the triumphal entry of the Emperor Constantine II into Rome in AD 357, he was preceded by dragon-standards carried aloft on gilded and jewelled spears.[10] These were not mere flags, but three-dimensional objects made from tubes of stiffened cloth, rather like the canvas windsocks of an airfield. The larger end was fixed onto a carved wooden or metal head with gaping jaws, which concealed some form of whistling device that caused them to hiss loudly as the wind blew into them; the thinner end formed a tail that lashed to and fro in the wind. An example can be seen carved on the Arch of Septimius Severus. One also reads of Persian, Parthian and Scythian armies having dragons on their banners. More relevantly to British history, some kings of Wessex used a dragon standard, Viking warships often had a dragon or serpent as a figurehead, and the Red Dragon was, and still remains, the national emblem of Wales. According to Geoffrey of Monmouth, Uther Pendragon (the father of King Arthur) had a dragon made of gold 'to carry about with him in the wars', and medieval heralds believed that his arms had been two green dragons, back to back. By a similar process of thought, some families and individuals chose a dragon as their heraldic device; Sir Francis Drake had one incorporated into the coat of arms granted to him by Elizabeth I, thus making a pleasing pun upon his name.

## The Northern Dragons

The Germanic and Scandinavian dragon tales, fascinating though they are, form a slightly isolated group, relatively untouched by the chief currents of medieval Christian thought. It is curious, for example, to notice that the writer of the Anglo-Saxon epic *Beowulf* carefully refrains from identifying his very impressive dragon with the Devil, despite the fact that this poet is unmistakably Christian in outlook and explicitly connects his other monster, Grendel, with the wicked descendants of Cain. In *Beowulf*, in the various German and Scandinavian versions of the story of Siegfried (Sigurd), and in certain Icelandic sagas where dragons play a part, the dragon is first and foremost a guardian of treasure; often it is the existence of this treasure, and in some cases a curse laid on it, which shapes the course of the story. But there are also other aspects of this Northern dragon-lore. Fafnir, whom Sigurd the Volsung (Siegfried) slew, was not only a treasure-guarding dragon but also a wise and magical being, whose flesh gave anyone who ate it the power to understand the language of birds, and whose blood conferred invulnerability. At the mythological level, Scandinavian cosmology preserves ancient themes in vivid form. There is the huge World Serpent coiled round the whole earth, which Thor the thunder god tries repeatedly to destroy, and which, with other monsters, will eventually rise up in fury to slay the gods and bring the present cycle of creation to its close; there is also a deadly serpent lurking at the roots of the World Tree, Yggdrasil, and perpetually seeking to gnaw it away. Versions of these cosmological myths may have been known to the pre-Christian English, but no allusions to them survive in Anglo-Saxon writings. In any case, the Norman Conquest broke whatever links remained with the Germanic world; Beowulf and Sigurd were forgotten in England, until such time as writers in the nineteenth and twentieth centuries rediscovered the power of these stern legends.

## Zoological Errors

So much for the dragons of cosmic myths, of hero-legends, of saints' legends, and of heraldry. But there has been another factor that has been at work until quite recent centuries, and that is the belief once soberly held by many writers on natural history in Classical times that remarkable reptiles of unusual size or attributes actually existed – though not in the writer's own country. There are statements of this sort in Pliny, Aristotle, Herodotus, and Aelian, referring to dragons huge enough to master an elephant and drain its blood, to sea serpents that will attack a trireme, to Egyptian winged serpents which fly about in swarms and are particularly addicted to the frankincense tree, and to other similarly sensational creatures. These writers carried immense prestige in later centuries. In view of their authority, and that of the Biblical allusions to dragons, one cannot really blame medieval scholars for including dragons, basilisks, and various weird types of serpent in their bestiaries. Late but excellent specimens can be found in Ulisse Aldrovandus, *Serpentum et Draconum Historiae*, 1640, and Edward Topsell, *The Historie of Serpents*, 1608.

When post-Renaissance naturalists began the vast work of describing and classifying the types of living creatures, they were overshadowed by the authority of this tradition, and it was only by slow degrees and after much controversy that the time-honoured belief in mermaids, unicorns, phoenixes, dragons and so forth was discarded. The task was made more difficult by the existence of cunning fakes, the so-called 'Jenny Hanivers', that is to say cleverly dried and mounted 'specimens' made from the bodies of real animals of different species combined together and so distorted as to be unrecognisable. There were many of these in the European markets in the sixteenth and seventeenth centuries; the best known are the pseudo-mermaids, but pseudo-dragons certainly existed too. As Richard Carrington has pointed out:

> A number of peculiar objects which were probably Jenny Haniver dragons were seen in Paris by Hieronymus Cardarus, the great Italian

mathematician and physician of Pavia, as long ago as the sixteenth century. He described them as 'two-footed creatures with very small wings; which one could scarcely deem capable of flight, with a small head . . . like a serpent, of a bright colour, without any feather or hair.' The size of these odd little animals was about that of a small rabbit, and they were definitely regarded at the time as dragon babies. Several theories have been proposed to explain what these creatures actually were . . . We can probably assume that they were dried lizards with one pair of legs amputated and with bats' wings cunningly grafted onto their sides. The suggestion has also been made that they were mutilated specimens of the little flying lizard *draco volans* of the Malay Peninsula and the East Indies.[11]

Illustrations which appear to be based on similar fakes can be seen in the works by Aldrovandus and Topsell mentioned above. The former also includes a most weird and repulsive looking creature with a crested head, a 'flexible tail two feet in length bristling with prickles', and 'a skin like that of a skate'. This last phrase contains the vital clue, for this particular 'dragon' is recognisably a much distorted skate, its fins slit and raised to do duty as wings. No doubt there were also cruder specimens about, like the eels with frogs' heads sewn onto them which were exhibited in nineteenth-century fairs as baby sea serpents.

All in all, it is not surprising that it was only in the eighteenth century that scientists achieved a reasonable degree of certainty over what could and what could not exist by way of land animals, or that speculations about sea serpents and other water-monsters persisted through the nineteenth century, and are indeed still with us today. Fortified by the thought of the coelacanth, and armed with cameras and echo-sounders, the hopeful heirs of a long tradition still keep vigil on the banks of Loch Ness. Any report or rumour of a sighting rouses instant public excitement and curiosity, mixed with sceptical amusement. 'Good Old Nessie' is also an instantly recognisable figure available to any designer of posters, films, advertisements and the like, which can be counted on to evoke affection as well as laughter. It seems that most people, at least in Britain, enjoy the thought of monsters of this type, and would rejoice if by any chance it could be shown that they do exist after all.

# CHAPTER TWO

# Habits and Habitats of British Dragons

For most people, the typical characteristics of a dragon are his wings, his fiery breath, his remote dwelling (usually a cave), and the hoard of gold over which he jealously mounts guard. All these features are to be found superbly described in *Beowulf*, except that there the dwelling is a hollow, stony burial-mound:

> The age-old scourge that haunts the half-light
> Found what delights him, a hoard, unguarded.
> It is he who, blazing, seeks burial mounds,
> He, the smooth, spiteful dragon that flies through the night,
> Enveloped in flame; all men fear him greatly.
> He seeks out a hoard which lies hidden in earth,
> And there he abides – he is ancient and wise –
> Beside heathen gold. He gains nothing by this.[1]

From other passages in the poem we learn that the mound in which this dragon lurked undisturbed for three hundred years is on a rocky headland by the sea, remote from inhabited areas; a stream gushes out from it, its waters boiling hot from the dragon's fire. The creature itself is a huge serpent ('Worm') with wings, but no legs are mentioned; when angered by the theft of one of its treasures it flies far and wide, spewing fire onto human homes, but in single combat with Beowulf it makes no use of this power of flight. Its weapons are its hot breath and its sharp teeth; Beowulf's sword shatters against its hard head, but his companion pierces its belly, causing the fire within to die down, and Beowulf finally dispatches it by ripping it open with his knife. However, its bite had been venomous, and so the hero dies too, rejoicing in the treasure he has won and in having saved his people from destruction. Hero and dragon lie side by side in death:

> The killer too lay,
> The fearsome earth-dragon, bereft of his life,
> Struck down and destroyed. The crooked, coiled worm
> No longer could keep the rich hoard of rings,
> For the hard steely edge which hammers had forged,
> The blade notched in battle, had taken his life;
> He, the wide flier, by wounds was made still,
> And sank to the ground by his lair, full of gold.
> No more would he circle and swoop through the air
> At midnight, or make himself seen far and wide,
> Proud of his riches; he fell to the earth,
> Because of the strength of the warrior's arm.

## Treasure Guardians

One of the first questions that springs to mind when considering British local folktales of later centuries is whether this strong pre-Conquest association between dragons, burial mounds and hidden treasures has left any traces in them. There are some, but they are remarkably few, both in comparison with the total number of local dragon-tales and in comparison with the total number of burial mounds. A few barrows have or once had names revealing that at one time a tradition about dragons was attached to them, although no story now survives there. Such are 'Dragon Hoard', a name known since the thirteenth century for a barrow at Garsington (Oxfordshire); 'Drakelowe', recorded in 1582 as the name of an unidentified site near Wolverley (Worcestershire); Drakelow in Derbyshire, first mentioned in 772; and 'Drake Howe' in Bilsdale, North Yorkshire. At Walmsgate in Lincolnshire, the name of which is said to be a corruption of 'Wormsgate', there is a long barrow reputed to contain the bones of a dragon which was killed and buried there, but no gold is mentioned. There is a tradition about a winged serpent at a barrow at Trellech-ar-Bettws in Carmarthen, and since most Welsh stories about winged snakes talk of their gold and jewels we may assume a treasure here, though it is not explicitly mentioned.[2] Traditions about treasure-guarding dragons have also been recorded for Old Field Barrows in Shropshire, Wormelow Tump in Herefordshire, and Money Hill on Gunnarton Fell in Northumberland. Sometimes the association is not with mounds, but with stones; there was a Drake Stone or Dragon Stone in 1651 at Stinchcombe in Gloucestershire, and another Drake Stone at Anwick in Lincolnshire. The latter is a natural boulder, now broken in two; the story about it was recorded in 1931, by which time it seems that the old meaning of 'drake' had been forgotten, for the treasure-guardian as here described sounds like a mere male duck:

Local tradition says that a man was ploughing in the field known as Drake Stone Close, when he was horrified to find horses and plough fast disappearing into a sort of quicksand. He himself managed to keep on firm ground, but he could not get the horses out, try as he would. As the quicksand finally closed over them, with a horrid sucking noise, a drake seemed to fly out of the hole where the horses had disappeared, and flew away with a discordant quacking. Next morning he revisited the spot to find the ground firm, but a slight depression indicated the site of the tragedy, in the middle of which was a large boulder stone, something of the shape of a drake's head; since when this stone has been known as the Drake Stone. It was always said that under the stone there was a great deal of treasure hidden, and many were the efforts to obtain it on the quiet, but no one was successful . . . [one man tried to raise the stone but his chain broke] and the guardian spirit of the treasure flew from under the stone in the form of a drake, and back went the stone to its accustomed place again.[3]

In Devonshire there is a tradition which can be traced back to the early seventeenth century that a dragon flies every night across the Exe Valley from the hill-fort on Dolbury Hill to that on Cadbury, or vice versa, guarding treasures hidden on one or other or both. These are so great that a local rhyme boasts:

> If Cadbury Castle and Dolbury Hill down delved were,
> Then Denshire might plough with a golden coulter
> And eare with a golden share.[4]

In Sussex in the nineteenth century, it was said that a hoard of gold lay buried somewhere under the huge hill-fort of Cissbury; it could be reached by way of a two-mile underground passage, but nobody had succeeded because halfway along the tunnel a pair of monstrous serpents would drive off the intruder.[5] In Wales, the belief in treasure-guarding serpents was more widespread than in England, and seems to have been held with deeper conviction. In that region, however, such tales are not linked with ancient burial mounds or earthworks; instead, the Welsh winged serpents were said to haunt thick woods and lonely hills (see below pages 40–1).

It will be noticed that in all these traditions the contact between the dragons and human beings is minimal or non-existent; they do not devastate the countryside, nor does anyone attack them, let alone kill them. The whole point of the tale is that the treasure is still there, so near and yet unobtainable; consequently its guardian dragon is also pictured as being still there, though hidden and inactive unless disturbed. Conversely, in the many British legends about a local hero who once killed a dragon, there is never any treasure for him to take away from the monster's lair, although other types of reward may well come his way as a result of his prowess. The fundamental patterns governing treasure-legends and dragon-slaying legends in our folklore of recent centuries are in fact incompatible. The invariable pattern of a legend of buried treasure (examples of which can be found all over the country) is that a hoard of gold or a golden statue lies hidden in some well-known spot, but that some supernatural force defeats all those who have tried to get at it. Sometimes there is a taboo, which the seekers inevitably violate; sometimes the Devil shifts the treasure, or storms break out when anyone gets near; often it is guarded by a supernatural beast, which may be a dog, calf, goat, raven or cock, and this beast terrifies all seekers and drives them away. This is the pattern into which the drake of Anwick, the Exe Valley dragon and the snakes of Cissbury all fit, and this is why they are never defeated and their treasure remains unrobbed. The ancient Germanic theme of the warrior who wins a dragon's hoard has vanished from more modern British lore.

## Luck-bringing Snakes

In nineteenth-century Wales, however, we find some remarkable survivals of an even more ancient theme, the Graeco-Roman cult of the protective luck-bringing snake, the god of the family in serpent form. A few anecdotes printed by Marie Trevelyan in 1909 illustrate this:

> In quiet and leafy neighbourhoods snakes have been known to go to children when alone, and sip milk with them out of their basins and mugs, and a friendship has been formed between them . . . An ancient farmhouse in the Vale of Taff was frequented by a King Snake and his courtiers. While these serpents remained in their old haunts all went well, and prosperity continued. But when the farmer died, his eldest son immediately killed the King Snake, whereupon the others took their departure. With them went the health, happiness and prosperity of the farm for ever.
>
> A Vale of Glamorgan story runs thus: To a farmer's daughter near Penmark a large snake used to come at milking time. The girl noticed that it wore a crown on its head. Every morning and evening the girl used to give the snake some warm new milk. One day the snake vanished, but it left a ring of gold on the spot where it used to come night and morning. It was whispered that the girl substituted this ring for the marriage circlet on her wedding day, and that by that means she became very rich . . . In some parts of the Principality there was formerly a tradition that every farmhouse had two snakes, a male and a

female. They never appeared until just before the death of the master or mistress of the house; then the snakes died.[6]

These benevolent Welsh snakes have features in common with the flying serpents believed in in the same areas (see page 40), notably that there are among them kings with jewelled crests or crowns, and that they own gold. They thus provide an unexpected and fascinating link between the ancient Classical belief in the holy and luck-bringing snake and the more wide-spread concept of the dangerous treasure-guarding dragon.

## Voracious Dragons

In the rest of Britain's legends, however, there is nothing to link dragons with luck and helpfulness to men. Instead we find tales which imply – or more often explicitly state – that they are aggressive beasts of prey whose normal occupation is to devour livestock from nearby pastures, and who will readily eat human beings too, if these should come their way. There is no need to provoke them; destructive activities are their natural way of life, and so there will be no peace for anyone until they are hunted down and killed.[7] This theme may be treated seriously, as in the Orkney tale of the Stoor Worm:

> His breath was so venomous that when he was angry and blew out a great blast of it every living thing within reach was destroyed and all the crops were withered. With his forked tongue he would sweep hills and villages into the sea, or seize and crush a house or ship so that he could devour the people inside.

Or it may be given a more comic tone, as in a Sussex story (see Appendix A):

> Thisyer ole dragon, you know, he uster go spanneling [traipsing] about the Brooks by night to see what he could pick up for supper, like – few horses, or cows maybe – he'd snap 'em up as soon as look at 'em. Then bimeby [by-and-by] he took to sitting atop o' Causeway, and anybody come along there, he'd lick 'em up, like a toad licking flies off a stone.

But everywhere the essential point is the same, that dragons are dangerous and destructive creatures. Sometimes they prey particularly on children, as did one at Moston in Cheshire, which Sir Thomas Venables shot in the eye just as it was about to swallow a little child; the family crest of the Venables is a dragon with a child in its jaws. In three or four cases, it is specified that the dragon preys upon young maidens in a manner reminiscent of Greek legends and, more immediately relevant, of the international fairytale 'The Dragon Slayer' (or, as it is entitled in the

Grimms' version, 'The Two Brothers.') One example of this is the Orkney tale of 'Assipattle and the Stoor Worm', already cited above, in which 'the only way to keep the Stoor Worm happy was to feed him on young virgins, seven of them each week . . . Every Saturday morning seven terrified girls were bound hand and foot and laid on a rock beside the shore. Then the monster raised his head from the sea and seized them in the fork of his tongue and they were seen no more.' Another Scottish tale combines the killing of girls with the very archaic trait of a dragon that forbids access to water, the mythological importance of which was noted in Chapter 1; a nineteenth-century summary tells us:

> Near Dundee, in Forfarshire, there is a well called the Nine Maidens' Well, and adjoining are places named respectively Pittempton, Baldragon, Strathmartin and Martinstane. From these simple circumstances we have a dragon story, which may be thus abridged. A dragon devoured nine maidens at the well near Pittempton. Martin, the lover of one of the maidens, finding life a burden, determined to kill the reptile or perish in the attempt. Accordingly he attacked it with a club, striking the first blow at Strath- (pronounced by the country people 'Strike-') martin. The venomous beast was scotched, not killed, by this blow; but as it dragged (in Scots, 'draiglet') its slow length along through a morass, the hero of the adventure followed up the attack, and finally killed the monster at Martinstane. The dragon, like other great criminals of the olden time, made 'a last speech and confession and dying declaration' in the following words:
>
> > I was tempit at Pittempton,
> > Draiglet at Baldragon,
> > Striken at Strikemartin,
> > And killed at Martinstane.[8]

An earlier summary of this story, in *The Statistical Account of Scotland* (1793) supplies the interesting detail that the girls were all sisters 'who had gone out, on a Sunday evening, one after the other, to fetch spring-water to their father.' Evidently, this dragon guarded the well against intruders; but equally evidently the Scottish storytellers, not finding this a satisfactory or comprehensible element in the tale, supplied a further motive more meaningful to them: it was *Sunday* evening, so the girls were breaking the Sabbath by working, and (by implication) deserved their fate.

The theme of water recurs more prominently in the story of the Dragon of Longwitton (Northumberland):

> In a wood not far from the village of Longwitton are three wells which have been famous for many years. Long ago, people used to travel from

far and near to drink water from the wells, for it was as sweet as wine, and had great healing powers . . . One day, however, a ploughman, going to quench his thirst, was alarmed to find a huge dragon there. It had coiled its tail round one of the trees, and pushed its long black tongue into the well, and was lapping the water like a dog . . . From that day, no pilgrim dared visit the magic wells, for the dragon haunted them. It was fearsome monster, with a skin as warty as a toad's, and a long tail like a big lizard's. It tore up the ground with its claws, and scraped the bark from the trees as it brushed past them . . . It seemed to have claimed the wells and would not give them up to anyone.[9]

Yet, paradoxically, these terrible monsters are sometimes said to be addicted to the mildest and most innocent of drinks, a supply of fresh milk. This is, in fact, an aspect of their serpent nature; in many regions, including Sweden, Greece and India, it has been commonly believed that snakes are fond of milk, and that a saucer of it should be put out for them. During the Middle Ages in Europe, it was thought that a snake can suck milk directly from a cow's udders, or even from a woman's breast. One of our most detailed dragon legends, that of the Lambton Worm (see Appendix A), lays particular stress on milk; every day a trough must be filled with the milk of nine cows, as the only way of preventing the monster's depredations.[10]

The popular song based on this same story represents the worm as getting his supplies by his own efforts, presumably by sucking the cows' udders:

> Now t'worm got fat an' growed an' growed,
>     And growed an awful size,
> He'd great big teeth, a great big gob,
>     And great big goggly eyes.
> And when at night he'd crawled around
>     To pick up bits of news
> If he felt dry upon the road,
>     He milked a dozen cows.

As we shall see in a later chapter, this love of milk actually proved the undoing of three dragons in other parts of England.

## Physical Characteristics

Other characteristics often alluded to are the dragon's poisonous and/or fiery breath and his tendency to lash his body against a foe or coil around him in the manner of a boa constrictor. His wings and power of flight are often mentioned in the initial description, but (as in *Beowulf*) play no part in the subsequent combat. Flying dragons[11] are commonest in Welsh legends, where they may have been influenced by a vigorous and long-lasting Welsh belief in the actual existence of winged snakes, about which Marie Trevelyan writes:

> The woods round Penllyne Castle, Glamorgan, had the reputation of being frequented by winged serpents, and these were the terror of old and young alike. An aged inhabitant of Penllyne, who died a few years ago [i.e. about 1900], said that in his boyhood the winged serpents were described as very beautiful. They were coiled when in repose, and 'looked as if they were covered with jewels of all sorts. Some of them had crests sparkling with all the colours of the rainbow.' When disturbed they glided swiftly, 'sparkling all over,' to their hiding places. When angry, they 'flew over people's heads, with outspread wings bright, and sometimes with eyes too, like the feathers in a peacock's tail.' He said it was 'no old story invented to frighten children,' but a real fact. His father and uncle had killed some of them, for they were 'as bad as foxes for poultry.' The old man attributed the extinction of the winged serpents to the fact that they were 'terrors in the farmyards and coverts.'
>
> An old woman, whose parents in her early childhood took her to visit Penmark Place, Glamorgan, said she often heard the people talking about the ravages of the winged serpents in that neighbourhood. She described them in the same way as the man of Penllyne. There was a 'king and queen' of winged serpents, she said, in the woods round Bewper. The old people in her early days said that wherever winged serpents were to be seen 'there was sure to be buried money or something of value' near at hand. Her grandfather told her of an encounter with a winged serpent in the woods near Porthkerry Park, not far from Penmark. He and his brother 'made up their minds to catch one, and watched a whole day for the serpent to rise. Then they shot at it, and the creature fell wounded, only to rise and attack my uncle, beating him about the head with its wings.' She said a fierce fight ensued between the men and the serpent, which was at last killed. She had seen its skin and feathers, but after the grandfather's death they were thrown away. That serpent was as notorious 'as any fox' in the farmyards and coverts around Penmark. Buried money had been found not far from Penmark Place in her childhood, and she said it had been 'hidden away by someone before going to the great Battle of St Fagan's, when the river ran red with blood.'

These Welsh creatures are exceptional in British dragon-lore for several reasons; not only are they apparently smaller than the usual conception of a dragon, more beautiful, and with uniquely bird-like features, but they are also thought of as a numerous species, not solitary individuals. The traditions about them oddly combine colourfully exotic descriptions with the mundane attitude of a farmer or gamekeeper towards vermin.

At one time flying dragons were also part of Devonshire beliefs, as Theo Brown notes:

> Two seventeenth century historians mentioned 'dragons' at Winkleigh. Westcote (1630) said that 'divers hillocks of earth' at Challacombe on Exmoor were supposed to have fiery dragons flying and alighting on them. Polwhele, in 1798, spoke sarcastically of a giant snake killed near a tin-mine at Manaton, credited with wings and legs and the size of a human body – and a hiss which could be heard for miles around – which had been seen to fly to and fro. This all seems derived from an antique period when
> The gaunt wolf and winged serpent held
> Dominion o'er the vale.

Essex too had a 'flying serpent', though the creature may owe its existence more to catchpenny journalism than to genuine folk traditions; it made its appearance in a pamphlet published in Clerkenwell in 1669, entitled *A True Relation of a Monstrous Serpent seen at Henham on the Mount in Saffron Walden*. It was alleged to have been eight or nine feet long, as thick as a man's leg, with large eyes, fierce teeth, and ridiculously small wings; it was supposedly sighted several times on 27 and 28 May 1669, doing no harm to anyone, and then disappeared into nearby woods. This pamphlet is thought to have been written by Robert Winstanley of Saffron Walden, compiler of the popular *Poor Robin's Almanac*; certainly the *Almanac* kept the story going in later years by anniversay entries, e.g. '1672: Four years since the serpent flew at Henham'; '1674: On 30 May a fair is held at Henham for the sale of Flying Serpents.' The publicity attending this tale, and the fair, may account for the existence of two London pubs called 'The Essex Serpent', but nevertheless the legend seems to lack roots in local tradition; possibly it was inspired simply by a medieval carving of a dragon in St Mary's Church, Henham.

However, there are plenty of local storytellers who disregard the flying powers of dragons; for them, these creatures are essentially super-snakes that crawl and coil and swim, for which the name of 'worm' so commonly used in Scotland and the North is indeed the most appropriate term. The question of legs is more debatable, some verbal descriptions including them and others not. Pictorial representations, on the other hand, whether medieval or more modern, almost always do include them; indeed, legs are an essential item in the heraldic definition of a dragon, the four-legged species being true dragons and the two-legged ones wyverns. In any case, once the story is under way the legs are not often mentioned; we do not commonly hear of dragons gripping heroes with their claws, nor of heroes maiming dragons by cutting their feet off. One exception to this is at Castle Carlton in Lincolnshire, where the monster's right thigh is of particular importance:

> With its long scaly body, short iron-clad legs, lashing tail, and head in which was set one blazing eye the size of a basin, it struck terror into the boldest heart. Nor was its body vulnerable, save where a small wart stood out on its right thigh – to pierce this would kill it, but a triple guard of brass protected the spot.[12]

Another variable feature is size. Often this is indicated only by some vague term such as 'huge', and each hearer may visualise for himself whatever seems the appropriate size – large enough to be a fearsome foe, but not so large as to make combat quite impossible. But this vagueness may sometimes be due simply to the second-hand summarised accounts in which so many of these tales survive. When we have detailed narratives presented by collectors who have really troubled to listen to local story-tellers, we find that the vivid awareness of local topography usually brings with it an equally vivid precision in the way the dragon is set against the physical background. Thus we read, in the best version of 'The Knucker of Lyminster' (Sussex), that 'there was ole Knucker [i.e. the dragon] lying just below Bill Dawes's place – least, his head was, but his neck and body-parts lay all along up the hill, past the station, and he was a-tearing up the trees in Batworth Park with his tail.' Examination of the terrain indicates that the Knucker must therefore have been at least half a mile long. The Lambton Worm must have been considerably longer, since the song informs us:

> An' when he'd eaten all he could
> An' he had had his fill,
> He'd crawl away and lap his tail
> Ten times round Lambton Hill.

The pamphlet version of this legend (See Appendix A) notes that this hill, which is also known as Worm Hill, bears marks made when the dragon squeezed it in his coils. The same explanation for ridges on a hill is given at Bignor (Sussex), Linton and Cnoc-na-Cnoimh (Sutherland), the name of which is Gaelic for 'Worm's Hill'. But all these monsters, big as they are, are dwarfed by the fantastic Orkney sea-dragon, the 'muckle mester Stoor Worm' who was 'so long that there was no place for his body until he coiled it round the earth', and whose corpse formed the island of

Iceland – truly, a worthy descendant of the Midgardsorm of Scandinavian myth! This particular story, however, which is given in Appendix A, is not really typical of local legends; it belongs more to the world of fairytale, of lowly heroes and lovely princesses, of magic horses and fantastic monsters. Local legends pitch their tone a little lower, and are rather more carefully rooted in the soil of everyday life.

One power which the legends sometimes ascribe to a dragon does at first sight seem sheer fantasy, namely his ability to rejoin severed portions of his body and resume the combat unharmed. But this is no more than the projection, onto dragon-scale, of a power which many country people believed they had observed in worms and reptiles; everyone knows that a lizard can grow a new tail or leg to replace one that has been broken off, many gardeners used to think that a worm cut in two by the spade will rejoin, and the way in which a crushed or severed snake will go on wriggling for hours gave rise to a saying that snakes cannot die before sundown. So if lizards, worms and snakes can do it, why not dragons? It is not a totally weird concept like the medieval amphisboena (a snake with a head at both ends) or the hundred-headed hydra – exotic creatures that one cannot readily imagine as lying with their heads 'just below Bill Dawes's place'.

Similarly, the intensely venomous breath often mentioned has its parallel in the allegedly destructive powers of snakes' breath, which, though quite without factual basis, were still being discussed in modern times.[13] Thus in 1828, Chateaubriand wrote of a certain American snake: 'Great caution is necessary not to enter the atmosphere which surrounds it. It decomposes the air which, imprudently inhaled, induces langour. The person wastes away, the lungs are affected, and in the course of four months he dies of consumption.' Even in 1909, Major Percy Fawcett claimed that a huge serpent he had shot near the Amazon had an appalling smell, 'probably its breath, which is believed to have a stupefying effect, first attacking and then paralysing the prey'. Against this background, the deadly breath ascribed to the Mordiford Dragon and the dragon of Cnoc-na-Cnoimh (see pages 68–9, 87) can be easily understood as one more instance of the dragon as super-snake.

## Birth and Infancy

Almost all the stories deal only with the full-grown solitary dragon, beginning their accounts at the stage where he is already a menace to the country around; the tellers did not usually concern themselves with questions as to where dragons come from or how they multiply. But there are several exceptions to this generalisation, each one proffering a different theory, and each fascinating in itself.

At Norton Fitzwarren (Somerset), it is said that a certain dragon was generated 'by a process not unlike spontaneous combustion' from a pile of dead bodies on a battlefield (see page 57). 'Spontaneous generation' would be a more accurate term, for the notion clearly derives from a long-outmoded scientific theory that certain animals are formed by the action of heat on decaying flesh. As so often, what had once been orthodox medical or scientific teaching lingers on at popular level long after it has been proved an error; in this instance, the error has an ancient and respectable history, being alluded to by many Classical and medieval writers. There is a particularly relevant passage in Plutarch's *Life of Cleomenes of Sparta*. The corpse of Cleomenes was found with a large snake (*drakon*) coiled round it and protecting it from birds of prey; some people said that this showed he had been dear to the gods and of more than mortal nature, while others argued that 'as oxen when they putrefy breed bees, and horses wasps, and beetles come to life from decaying asses, so human carcasses when some of the juices about the marrow congeal and thicken give rise to serpents.' It is delightful to find the last remote echoes of this bit of pseudo-biology lingering in Somerset in a story recorded as recently as 1968.

Another theory about the origins of dragons was widely and strongly held in Wales until late in the nineteenth century. It was believed that if an ordinary snake ever happened to drink milk from a woman's breast, or to eat bread that had been consecrated for the Eucharist, it would undoubtedly turn into one of the dangerous flying snakes already described above, or, worse still, into a *gwiber*.[14] This word is etymologically the same as 'viper', but in Welsh it could mean a monstrous snake, huge, winged, and scaly, which was very much dreaded. For this reason, people would be angry if a woman whose breasts were too full eased herself by milking them onto the ground; she might be responsible for the appearance of a *gwiber*.

Two local legends which take an interest in the infancy though not the actual birth of dragons are the story of the Lambton Worm and one version of that of the Mordiford Dragon.[15] Both stress the apparent harmlessness of the creature when it is first found at a young and helpless stage, and the dangers of allowing it to grow up. The story from Mordiford (Hereford-shire) is one of those collected by J. Dacres Devlin for his little book on *The Mordiford Dragon*, which was published in 1848; it was told him by an old man in his nineties, who lived in the next village, Hampton Bishop. According to this, a little girl called Maud found a baby dragon in the woods, which was bright green and about the size of a cucumber; she took it home, much to the horror and fury of her parents, who said it was a wicked creature which she should on no account keep. She pretended to obey, but in fact she kept it hidden and managed to go on feeding it secretly on milk, which it liked very much. It grew fast, and once it was fully grown its tastes changed and it became carnivorous; at first it took poultry, then sheep, then cows, and finally human beings. But it remembered Maud's kindness, and was always gentle and tame with her.

It would be easy to fit a moral to a story like this. At Lambton Castle in County Durham, moralising is applied in full force to the prose version of the local tale, which is the most explicitly 'preachy' among British dragon legends. The hero, a dissolute and profane young man, goes fishing on a Sunday, and adds to this sacrilege by swearing when he fails to catch anything. Shortly after, he feels something on his hook:

> But what was his surprise and mortification when, instead of a fish, he found he had only caught a worm of most unseemly and disgusting appearance, and he hastily tore it from his hook and threw it into a well hard by . . . The stranger saw the worm, and remarked that he had never seen the like of it before – that it was like an eft, but that it had nine holes on each side of its mouth, 'and tokened no good'.

The reference to an eft (that is, a newt) is interesting, and may be compared to one elaboration or offshoot of the Mordiford story. Apparently, in the 1870s, a Rector of Mordiford once found two old women in his church doing their best to drown a couple of newts in the font, because, so they said, these creatures were dragon spawn, and would grow up into monsters if they were not dealt with at once[16]. This is of course a joke; newts are aquatic, so the idea of someone trying to drown them is just a variation on a traditional jest about how some fool decided to punish an eel (or crab, or other aquatic creature) by throwing it into the sea to drown. But there does also seem to have been a real fear and dislike of newts among country people, harmless though they are; it was said that if you swallowed their spawn when drinking from a pond they would breed inside your stomach, taking all the goodness of your food, so that you would waste away. Possibly it was this fear of newts which led storytellers to choose them, rather than the more obviously dangerous adders, as candidates for the role of baby dragon – plus, of course, the fact that newts have feet, as do the heraldic dragons, wyverns and cockatrices.

## The Cockatrice

Here we may turn aside briefly to consider a lesser relative of dragons, the cockatrice or basilisk, which was included in medieval bestiaries on the authority of Classical writers, and passed into both heraldry and folklore. The word 'cockatrice', which is derived by way of a curious series of misunderstandings and corruptions from a Greek word for the ichneumon, influenced both the form in which it is represented and the tales told about it. In heraldry it is shown as having the legs and head of a cock, but its body merges into the tail of a serpent or small dragon; it is said not only to be extremely venomous, but to be able to kill people simply by looking at them with its deadly eyes. The birth of the creature is as curious as its form; it is said to be hatched out when a serpent or a toad sits upon an egg laid not by a hen but by a cock.

There is, surprisingly, a grain of truth in this fanciful picture, at least as regards the behaviour of the 'cock'. It is fairly common for poultry to suffer disturbances of their hormone balance, and when this occurs in a hen she develops noticeable external masculine features; she grows a comb, takes to crowing, fights off any cock that attempts to tread her, and herself tries to tread other hens. However, she still lays eggs, though as she is no longer mating they are of course infertile. In former times, this whole phenomenon was viewed with the unreasoning fear and disgust which unusual sexual behaviour so easily rouses, and the resulting 'cock's eggs' were believed to produce the baleful cockatrice with its death-dealing glance. But there was a way of coping with cockatrices, as Edward Topsell remarked in 1608:

I cannot without laughing remember the old wives' tales of the vulgar cockatrices that have been in England, for I have oftentimes heard it confidently related, that once our nation was full of cockatrices, and that a certain man did destroy them by going up and down in glasse, whereby their own shapes were reflected upon their own faces, and so they died.

A story of much the same type as amused Topsell once existed at Saffron Walden in Essex, where a knight is said to have donned a coat of 'cristal glass' in order to destroy a cockatrice by its own power. A similar tale is still current in Hampshire, about a cockatrice at Wherwell:

. . . it was said to have been hatched by a toad incubating a duck's egg in a dark dungeon beneath Wherwell Priory. At first the strange beast was merely an object of curiosity, but as the years passed it became a voracious monster whose appetite could only be satisfied by human flesh. A reward of four acres of land was offered to anyone who could slay the beast, and many brave men died in attempting the task. Finally an ingenious man named Green lowered a mirror of polished steel into the cockatrice's underground den. Regarding its own reflection as an enemy, the cockatrice battered itself against the mirror until eventually it slid to the ground exhausted. Avoiding the beast's gaze, Green then descended to the dungeon and killed the cockatrice with his spear. It is curious that for years the people of Wherwell could not be persuaded to eat a duck's egg, and further, that there is a four-acre plot of land in nearby Harewood Forest known as Green's Acres. The figure of a cockatrice that once topped the steeple of St Peter and Holy Cross at Wherwell is now in Andover Museum.[18]

There is another story about the outwitting of a cockatrice, there described as a many-eyed serpent, at Castle Gwys (see page 79); but the method is a different one.

## Habitats

Having now reviewed the habits and appearance of various British dragons, we must ask: what of their habitats? First of all, it is necessary to point out the error of a statement once made by William Henderson in his *Notes on the Folklore of the Northern Counties of England and the Border* (1879), since this is still sometimes accepted and repeated without further inquiry. After discussing various dragon-slaying legends in County Durham and Roxburgh, Henderson commented:

> Whether dragon-stories extend further into Scotland I cannot say, further than that one is current at Strathmartin, in Forfar . . . Certainly these tales appear circumscribed within a narrow district. I cannot hear of anything analogous to them in the South of England . . . [19]

This is very misleading; there are dragon tales in many southern and midland counties, though of course some of them had not been gathered into print in Henderson's time, while others were available only in books of purely local interest which he can be forgiven for not having seen. Excellent examples have been recorded in Devon, Essex, Gloucestershire, Hampshire, Herefordshire, Hertfordshire, Somerset, Suffolk and Sussex, not to mention Wales (see Appendix B for the full list known to me.) It would however be fair to say that they seem to be characteristic of either coastal areas or of river valleys, and preferably of areas where hills are fairly low; they are not to be found along the Pennines, and only very rarely on high moors and fells. However, this distinction breaks down in Wales, where traditions about dragons also occur in mountainous regions. In any case, generalisations like this are risky; for one thing, there may well be more legends still unknown to me, and for another, a distribution-map of folklore items is at least as likely to reflect the distribution of energetic collectors as that of the items being sought.

In the tales gathered in the present book, the variety of habitats ascribed to dragons is quite wide, and several stories mention more than one; for example, the creature may have his lair in a wood, or more rarely a cave, but be in the habit of seeking out a particular river to drink, and be slain at that spot. There is in fact a remarkable preponderance of water in all its forms – river, well, pool, lake, marsh, bog and sea. We have already met the

Orkney Stoor Worm, whose home was the seabed; the Lambton Worm who was fished out of the river Wear and eventually met his end there; the 'drake' at Anwick who flew up out of a boggy pit; the dragons who prevented access to wells at Strathmartin and Longwitton; the one with the warty leg at Castle Carlton, who lived inland but was killed by the sea; the Knucker of Lyminster (Sussex), who lived in a deep pool and went hunting along the marshy Arun Valley; the Mordiford Dragon, who in some versions (but not all) was killed beside the River Lugg; and the child-eating one at Moston (Cheshire), who lived in a pool. The Welsh flying serpents sometimes haunt waterfalls and wells, while at Llyn Cynwch near Dolgellau a wyvern would crawl out of the lake and up into the mountains, where it was eventually decapitated by a young shepherd with an axe.[20] In one way or another, water is also a feature of the habitats of dragons at Deerhurst (Gloucestershire), Brinsop (Herefordshire), Bamburgh (Northumberland), Wormingford (Essex), Bures (Suffolk), Aller (Somerset), Filey, Kellington and Wantley (Yorkshire), Dalry (Kirkudbright), and Ben Vair (Argyll), all of whose stories will appear in later pages.

In this connection, we cannot ignore the numerous lake-monsters and river-monsters in Scottish, Irish and Welsh traditions. They are of different forms; the majority are described as horses or cows; others as monsters combining a horse's head with the body of an eel, serpent or fish; others again as pure eels or snakes, but of huge dimensions.[21] Two Welsh anecdotes exemplify the latter type:

> The whirlpool of the River Taff at Cardiff forms a small lake when the bed is almost dry . . . People said it was fathomless, and that in its depths a monstrous serpent dwelt, and gorged on the unfortunate victims that were drowned in the river and sucked into the pool. When any bodies were not recovered from the whirlpool, people said they had been swallowed by the serpent . . .
>
> Llyn-y-Gader is a round lake in the south-west of Snowdon. A man of the eighteenth century swam across this lake, and his friends, watching him, noticed on his return that he was followed by a long, trailing object winding slowly after him. They were afraid to raise an alarm, but went forward to meet him as soon as he reached the shore where they stood. Just as he was approaching, the trailing object raised its head, and before anyone could render aid the man was enveloped in the coils of this monster, which dragged him to a deep hole in the end of the lake from which the Llyfin flows. There he was drowned, and the spot where he sank revealed blood-red waters.

A tale from Lady Gregory's collection, 1920, serves as an example of the Irish parallels:

The lake down there (Lough Graney) is an enchanted place and old people told me that one time they were swimming there, and a man had gone out into the middle, and they saw something like a great big eel making for him, and they called out 'If ever you were a great swimmer, show us now how you can swim to the shore,' for they wouldn't frighten him by saying what was behind him. So he swam to the shore, and he only got there when the thing behind him was in the place where he was. For there are queer things in lakes.

The most famous tale of this type is that in Adamnan's *Life of St Columba*, a seventh-century Latin text, which is frequently quoted as the earliest known sighting of the Loch Ness monster:

At another time . . . [Columba] found it necessary to cross the River Ness. When he comes to the bank, he sees some of the local people burying an unfortunate fellow whom – so those burying him claimed – some aquatic monster had shortly before snatched while he was swimming. The holy man orders one of his companions to swim out and bring over a cable moored on the other side. Hearing and obeying the command, Lugne Mocumin without delay takes off his clothes except his loincloth, and casts himself into the water. But the monster, perceiving the surface of the water disturbed by the swimmer, suddenly comes up and moves towards him as he was crossing the middle of the stream, and rushed up with a great roar and open mouth. The holy man seeing it . . . commanded the ferocious monster, saying 'Go thou no further nor touch the man. Go back at once.' Then on hearing this word of the saint the monster was terrified and fled away again more quickly than if it had been dragged on ropes, though it had approached Lugne as he swam so closely that between man and monster there was no more than the length of one punt pole.

To pursue these snake-like lake monsters in further detail would lead too far afield; suffice it to say that even though they are not actually called 'dragons' or 'worms' their alleged appearance and habits do resemble those of water-dwelling dragons in local legends, and the belief in their reality (which can be traced back for centuries and is not wholly extinct even nowadays in Ireland) would have been favourable to the growth of dragon legends. Unlike dragons, however, they are not the subjects of slaying stories; the point of most anecdotes about them is simply that they have been seen, and are (or may be) still lurking in their lakes.

It is certainly curious that local dragon-stories should so often include a mention of water in one form or another, but it may be unwise to read too much significance into it. Admittedly, as has been often pointed out by comparative mythologists, the dragons of ancient myth are constantly and intimately linked with water. This is true not only of Vṛtra, Tiamat and Leviathan/Lotan, but also of the benevolent rain-giving dragons of China and Japan. But though scholars are struck by such parallels, it seems to me most unlikely that British storytellers themselves ascribed any importance to the wells, rivers, pools and so forth mentioned in their accounts, beyond the simple pleasure of relating the tales as closely as possible to well-known features in the neighbourhood. The wells at Longwitton (for example, see page 38–9), were famous in their own right for their curative powers, and so were a convenient landmark around which to build a story. Again, one variant of the Mordiford story mentions a flood in the River Lugg – but simply in order to explain how the dragon, who according to that informant lived mostly in the river, gorged itself on a half-drowned ox and fell asleep, enabling all the villagers to creep up and surround it while it was sleeping, and hack it to pieces.[22] This is typical of how folktale imagination works; the keynote is practicality, not archaic myths and a consciousness of destructive forces in Nature.

As regards other habitats, woods and hills are frequently mentioned, and are always those that are quite close to the village where the tale is told, not remote or wild regions; the same applies to the fields, holes, caves and ruined buildings which may also occur in the story. Several burial-mounds were listed in connection with the discussion of treasure-guarding dragons earlier in this chapter, and we may add the 'hillocks' at Challacombe which are in fact a group of barrows. There is also a story about a dragon at Dalry (Kirkudbright) which Andrew Lang collected in 1885.[23] When it was first published, Lang said the creature's lair was a tumulus, but later he corrected himself and stated that the site, Mote Hill, was that of a Norman fort. There are one or two eccentric locations – corn stacks at Ben Vair in Argyll, and a church tower at Llandeilo Graban in the Wye valley, on which a dragon roosted by night after terrorising the district by day.[24] Maybe the explanation for this oddity is that the church had at one time had a weathervane shaped like a dragon (cf. the cockatrice weathervane at Wherwell in Hampshire); such objects easily become focal points for legend-building.

The absence of certain types of habitat also deserves careful note. With only one exception, there is no connection between dragons and those sites which are traditionally regarded as haunted, sinister or demonic, such as graveyards, gallows and gibbets, places where murders or suicides have occurred, and so forth. The exception is Lang's huge serpent at Dalry, which is said to have had the gruesome habit of stealing corpses from a churchyard and devouring them. Nor are there many associations between dragons and prehistoric stone circles or other megalithic monuments, the only cases of this being the dragon killed at Martinstane, which is a standing stone with Pictish carvings on it, and one which beat itself to death against a standing stone in Denbighshire (see page 83). The link between dragons and hill-forts applies mostly to treasure-guarding ones, and is best seen as a secondary development from the well-attested association between tales of buried treasure and prehistoric earthworks. However, the dragon of Norton Fitzwarren (Somerset), which was slain by Fulk Fitzwarren (page 57), is also said to have lived in a fort nearby. From these negative observations we may conclude, firstly, that dragons were not categorised as part of the eerie world of supernatural spirits and demons that lurk in haunted, evil places; secondly, that they were not associated in people's minds with the very remote and mysterious past evoked by prehistoric sites, but that they were thought of as having been 'right here, and not so very long ago'.

The sense of precise localisation is very strong in these stories, at any rate if they have been recorded with plenty of detail, and not just dismissively summarised or, alternatively, dressed up in a flavourless garb of conventional chivalry. In the best versions (as indeed in good local legends of all types), one finds a series of vivid and minutely particularised links between the story and its setting – where the dragon had his lair, where he hunted, where he came to drink, what paths he followed, where the hero lay in wait for him and killed him, and even, in one case, which pub the hero went to to celebrate afterwards:

> Jim Pulk was a farmer's boy, who baked a huge Sussex pie and put poison inside it, and drew it on a farm cart near to the Knucker Hole [at Lyminster], while he himself hid behind a hedge. The Dragon came out, ate the pie, died, and Jim Pulk then emerged and cut off his head with his scythe. He then went to the Six Bells Inn, had a drink to celebrate his victory, and fell down dead. Presumably he had got some poison on his hand, which, no doubt, very properly, he drew across his mouth after downing his pint.[25]

The places mentioned in the course of the stories are not usually of great intrinsic interest, though of course very familiar to the audience. One which does deserve examination for its own sake is this same pool at Lyminster (Sussex), known as the Knucker Hole. It is a pond locally reputed to be bottomless, though in fact it is about thirty feet deep, and it is fed from below by a strong underground source, so that it never freezes over, nor does the water-level ever vary, even in an intense drought like that of 1976. At one time, there were several such pools along the coastal plain of Sussex, though the others have now all been drained off or tapped for water-supplies; they were all known as 'Knucker Holes' or 'Nickery

Holes'. This word has a remarkable history; far from being meaningless, as it now seems, it is derived from an Anglo-Saxon word *nicor*, which means 'water-monster' and occurs in *Beowulf*. After the Conquest, it survived in dialects in various forms ('nicker', 'nucker', 'knucker'), and was used as an element in minor place-names, always to indicate pools, ditches, or deep places in a riverbed; in folklore, it also sometimes occurs as an element in the names of ogres or monsters that inhabit water. The fact that this word is applied to the Lyminster pool must mean that the pool was believed to contain a monster of some sort centuries ago, and indeed very likely in pre-Conquest times. Since the dragon at Lyminster is actually called 'Knucker' as his proper name, it looks as if the meaning of the word was accurately remembered there for many generations, though now forgotten. Thus the versions of the story recently current are only comparatively modern variations on a theme which must have persisted in this village for over a thousand years; perhaps, in the early stages, Knucker was thought of as a water-snake that swallowed the drowned, like the one in the whirlpool at Cardiff. Be that as it may, in this case, the dragon's habitat tells us more than we would otherwise have known about the dragon himself – his very considerable age.

# CHAPTER THREE

## *The Hero: Knight or Churl?*

Just as the dragons of British folktales are more diversified than one expects, so too are the heroes who dispose of them. The mention of dragon-slaying rouses an instant picture in everyone's mind: there stands the dragon, menacing with tooth and claw, and there, hurtling bravely towards him, is a mounted knight in shining armour, wielding the chivalric weapons, sword or spear. On reflection, it seems that the main memories which go to make up this stereotype are the legend of St George, Spenser's description of the Red Cross Knight, a vague impression of King Arthur's knights and other medieval champions (although actually giants are far commoner than dragons as superhuman adversaries in Arthurian literature), and possibly the more remote figures of St Michael, Perseus, Beowulf and Sigurd/Siegfried. These nobly-born heroes and warrior-saints, represented in innumerable paintings, book illustrations, statues and stained glass windows, have shaped our expectations concerning dragon-slayers; and St George at least would have been universally familiar at all periods since his cult first came to England during the Crusades. His importance in the development of processional and civic dragon-effigies will be discussed in Chapter 6.

### Saints as Heroes

There are two places in England which claim the honour of being the very spot where George killed his dragon. One is Brinsop in Herefordshire, and it is obvious what gave rise to the association, since its church is dedicated to him and has a fine early medieval tympanum which shows him spearing the monster.[1] It may also be relevant that the next village is called Wormsley. The story, having taken root at Brinsop, has been enriched by that firm, precise and mildly comic stress upon local detail which is so typical of these tales; the dragon, it is said, lived inside Dragon's Well in Duck's Pool Meadow just to the south of the church, and the saint fought and killed him in a field called Lower Stanks.

The second site for St George's combat is more distinctive – indeed, it is unique. It is the chalk-carved figure of the White Horse at Uffington (formerly in Berkshire, now reclassified as in Oxfordshire).[2] Not far from the head of this carving is a small conical flat-topped hill, with a bare chalky patch on its summit and several chalky gulleys down its sides, which is known as Dragon Hill. The story goes that St George's combat took place there, and that the areas where no grass grows are those where the dragon's poisonous blood soaked into the ground; or, alternatively, that the reason they are bare is that the dragon lies buried under the hill. Some storytellers have claimed that the White Horse itself is not a horse at all, but the portrait of the slain monster, and that that is why it looks so very unlike a real horse; others have asserted that it is meant to represent St George's steed. There may be some patriotic symbolism underlying this legend. The Vale of the White Horse was the site of the Battle of Ashdown, King Alfred's most important victory against the Danes, and some local people gladly adopted a theory put forward by the antiquarian Wise in 1738 that King Alfred himself had had the horse carved to commemorate his triumph. Though George was not chosen as patron of England until long after Alfred's time, it might well have seemed appropriate to link his legend to the site of a battle that saved the nation. Whatever its inspiration, the story was well established in local tradition by the early eighteenth century. In *The Scouring of the White Horse*, Tom Hughes records a few verses by a shepherd called Job Cork who worked in that area and died in 1807, which include the lines:

> If it is true as I heard say
> King Gaarge did here the dragon slay,
> And down below on yonder hill
> They buried him, as I heard tell . . .

Another saintly dragon-slayer is St Leonard, who, like George, was much venerated by Crusaders. In real life, he was a French hermit who lived from about 485 to 650. Since he had once persuaded King Clovis to release some prisoners, people prayed to him for the safe homecoming of prisoners of war. In Sussex, a wooded area near Horsham has been called St Leonard's Forest ever since the thirteenth century, because it once contained a chapel dedicated to him; in popular tradition this has been transformed into the idea that the Saint had actually lived in the area himself.[3] It is said, moreover, that he once killed a dragon there after a long and arduous fight in which he lost much blood; in reward for his courage, God granted that patches of wild lilies of the valley would grow for ever where his blood had been spilt, and that as the songs of the nightingales had been distracting him from prayer, no nightingale would ever sing in the Forest again. Saint Leonard is not elsewhere regarded as a dragon-slayer, so it may be that this localised legend about him could have grown up simply because one village within the Forest bounds is called Dragon's Green. And as for the name of this village, it seems simply to have arisen because there was a family surnamed 'Dragons' living at nearby Roffey in 1296, who owned this estate.

In medieval Britain, there were many cults of saints who are now almost wholly forgotten, except by local antiquarians; several of them were historical figures from the earliest times of Christianity in these islands, who were later credited with various fantastic adventures drawn from the common stock of hagiographical lore. Slaying or banishing a dragon is one such stock adventure; it is ascribed to St Carantoc of Somerset and St Petroc of Cornwall, both saints of the early Celtic Church.[4] Carantoc, it is said, had a miraculous stone altar, which he once set afloat on the Severn Estuary, so that it might guide him to whatever spot God wished him to settle in:

> In those days Arthur and Catho reigned over that region, and Arthur had come there on his travels in order to find a certain huge and terrible serpent which had devastated many fields. Carantoc came and greeted Arthur, who gladly accepted a blessing from him, and the saint asked him if he had heard whereabouts his altar had come to shore. The King said, 'If my request were granted, I would tell you.' 'What request do you want to make?' asked the saint. The King said, 'That you should remove the serpent which is near here, if, as it seems, you are a servant of God.' Then the man of God went and prayed to the Lord; and the serpent came to him straight away with a great roar, like a calf running to its mother, and bowed its head before the servant of God like a slave obedient to his master, humble and gentle-eyed. And he put his stole round its neck, and led it away like a lamb. Its neck was like a bull's neck, and the stole would hardly go round it. In this way they went to the stronghold, and greeted King Catho, who received them kindly. The man of God led the serpent into the middle of the court, and some people tried to kill it, but the saint would not allow it to be killed . . . And the saint led it out of the gate of the stronghold and released it, ordering it to depart and never to dare harm anyone again.

As a result of this, Carantoc not only got back his wonderful altar, but was given the stretch of land beside a river mouth where it had come to land, and was allowed to build a church there. The version of the legend given above is translated from the medieval Latin text printed by Wynkyn de Worde in 1516; the story remains well known in Somerset, where the stronghold is identified as Dunster Castle, the dragon's lair as Ker Moor,

and the land granted to Carantoc as Carhampton. Recent oral versions
have been recorded in books by Kingsley Palmer, Berta Lawrence and Ruth
Tongue.

As for St Petroc, he had two encounters with dragons, one being a
sinister monster, but the other rather pathetic:

> In those days Tandurus reigned [in Western Britain], a man of fierce
> and cruel ways, who in his savage tyranny had gathered worms and all
> sorts of noxious serpents into a pit of water, in order to punish and
> torture thieves there. After he died, his son, who succeeded him,
> forbade the useof such tortures; thereupon the famished snakes rose to
> the surface in a tightly packed mass and gnashed one another with
> their vicious fangs, so that out of all their great number there remained
> but one alive – a horrible one with a huge body, which tore cattle and
> men to pieces in its gaping jaws and venomous mouth. The man of
> God came to this place, and after kneeling to pray in front of everyone
> he restored to life a man who had died, and ordered the monster to
> depart to a wilderness beyond the seas, and never to harm anyone
> again . . .
>
> [On another occasion] a certain large dragon which used to come
> wandering round [Petroc's] cell had a piece of wood lodged in his right
> eye, so, having voided out all its harmful venom, it hurried to the place
> where the saint was praying, and there it lay for three days with its head
> bowed, waiting for the saint's favour. By order of the blessed Petroc,
> the dragon was then drenched with a liquid which was sprinkled over
> it, mixed with dust from the paving stones; the strength of this
> medicine at once drew the piece of wood out of its eye, and it went
> back healed to its solitary lair.

## Heroes from Medieval Romances

Occasionally some colourful episode from secular medieval romance
reappears as a local legend. One example concerns Fulk(e) Fitzwarrin,
who was a historical personage of the time of King John and was outlawed
as a result of quarrels with that king. Fulk's outlawry was the starting-point
for a long rambling romance about him, which now survives only in a
French prose version probably dating to the reign of Edward I, though it is
known that an English poem about him also existed at one time. One of
Fulk's many adventures in foreign lands involved an odd sort of dragon:

> In Carthage he overcame a monster or dragon that lived upon human
> flesh in a mountain near the sea, which had carried off the daughter of
> the Duke of Iberie. The writer seems to have got well confused as to the

nature of this beast. When Fulk is fighting with it he describes a huge winged reptile like the traditional dragon of St George. Elsewhere, however, it appears as a half-human monster . . .It lived in a house upon the mountain with a great door, and the Duke's daughter told Fulk how 'when his hideous face and beard were smeared with blood, he would come to me and cause me to wash with clear water his face and his beard and his breast.' When he had killed the dragon, Fulk took the cool gold upon which alone it could sleep, because of the hot fire in its belly, and having returned the princess to her father, sailed back to England.[5]

This story is of fairytale type, with its ogre-like monster, the treasure, and the princess; moreover, it is set in an exotic distant land, and so stands apart from the local legends of this country. Fulk himself, however, was a real person, and there are still several branches of the Fitz-Warryn(e) family extant, some of them bearing a dragon as their crest – a fact which certainly would have had a bearing on the development of a family legend. Sure enough, in Somerset, which is one of the areas with which Fulk was personally connected, one finds a tradition about Fulk as dragon-slayer in which his deed is presented as a purely local event. Collecting tales there in 1968, Kingsley Palmer found:

> The village of Norton Fitzwarren, not far from Taunton, has a well established and particularly interesting tradition about a dragon, connected with remains of an encampment dating from Iron Age, Roman and Saxon times. It is situated immediately behind the present town. The dragon is said to have emerged from the camp after a fierce battle. There were piles of dead bodies, and, by a process not unlike spontaneous combustion, they generated the dragon, which terrorized the neighbourhood, causing great damage and loss of life. It was a local valiant, Fulk Fitzwarine, who came to the rescue, killing the monster and saving the people from further distress.

Though this tale has been so recently collected, it certainly must have a long and probably rather complicated history. As was pointed out in Chapter 2, its explanation of the dragon's existence embodies an ancient bit of pseudo-science which, like so many such things, remained acceptable until the gradual rise of modern biology in the seventeenth century; its hero is medieval, and the village's own name shows its links with his descendants. To add to the complications, there is in Norton Fitzwarren Church a carved and painted wooden rood-screen dating from about 1500 which has figures of human beings and a dragon carved on it, but its interpretation is difficult. It shows several persons, some wielding objects which seem to be traps or agricultural instruments; none is a knightly figure, as Fulk would be. Presumably it tells a different version of the local story, one with a group of plebeian heroes, such as will be discussed below in connexion with Aller (Somerset) or Bures (Suffolk), since it is by no means unusual for variations to coexist in the same place, even if one differs quite sharply from the other. There is no way of guessing at what date the single medieval knightly hero, Fulk, replaced the group of local figures shown on the rood-screen; all that can be said is that he is now remembered, while their identity and the details of their story are forgotten.

Another hero of medieval romance whose story was once widely popular was Sir Guy of Warwick; chapbook and ballad versions of his adventures continued to be printed as late as the eighteenth century.[6] He was, among other things, a slayer of monstrous animals, in particular a certain wild boar and (in later versions of the tale) the celebrated Dun Cow with which his name is now always associated. Although he does not generally figure as a dragon-killer, there is one account of Northumbrian folklore, dating from the early nineteenth century, which claims that it was Sir Guy of Warwick who slew the dragon that infested the Holy Wells of Longwitton (see pages 38–9). It may also be just worth mentioning that another hero of the same type, Sir Bevis of Hampton, is said to have killed a dragon in the course of adventures in foreign lands; however, as his exploit (unlike Fulk's) has never been transferred to an English local setting, it is really more a matter of literary tradition than of folklore.

One story which did make the transition from medieval romance to localised legend is that of the Laidly (i.e. Loathsome) Worm. This does not describe a slaying, but a spell and disenchantment, and it is found as a ballad, *Kemp Owyne*. It tells of a girl whose stepmother threw her over a crag into the sea, at the same time laying on her a curse which turned her into a monster:

> Her breath grew strang, her hair grew lang,
>     And twisted three times about the tree,
> And all the people, far and near,
>     Thought that a savage beast was she.

The curse also stipulated that the girl could be released from this shape – but only if one particular knight, Kemp Owyne, should kiss her three times. When one day he arrives at the crag, it is with the intention of slaying the monster, but instead she challenges him to kiss her, in a strange mixture of promises and threats:

> 'Here is a royal belt,' she cried.
>     'That I have found in the green sea,

And while your body it is on,
   Drawn shall your blood never be;
But if you touch me, tail or fin,
   I swear my belt your death shall be.'

Kemp gives her three kisses, and at each one her hair loosens a little from the tree; at the third, her human form returns, and he greets her as his true love. As for the curse, it recoils on the stepmother, who from then on must live in Wormeswood as a rough-haired four-footed monster. There are other ballads with similar plots. *Alison Gross* tells of a knight who rejects an ugly witch's advances and is then turned into a worm, though his devoted sister comes every Saturday to comb his hair at the foot of a tree; while in *The Laidly Worm and the Machrel of the Sea* both brother and sister are transformed, he to a worm and she to a mackerel, but only he is rescued from the spell.[7]

These ballads have a localised variant set at Spindleston Heugh, an impressive craggy rock near Bamburgh Castle in Northumberland. The legend there was widely known at the time when Sir Walter Scott was collecting material for his *Minstrelsy of the Scottish Borders*, but unfortunately he thought it too much like *Kemp Owyne* to be worth printing. It told of a girl transformed into a dragon by a stepmother who hated her for her beauty. Some verses were later published by a Vicar of Norham, the Rev. Mr Lamb, who claimed that he was merely transcribing from a manuscript written down in 1270 by a local ballad-singer, Duncan Fraser, who came from the Muckle Cheviot. It is more than dubious whether any such manuscript ever existed; certainly many of Mr Lamb's verses have an unmistakably Victorian ring about them which reveal them only too clearly as his own work, but on the other hand he may well have relied on genuine local tradition for the details of his plot. When describing the Worm, for example, he lists features easily paralleled in other folk-tales:

For seven miles east and seven miles west,
   And seven miles north and south,
No blade of grass was seen to grow,
   So deadly was her mouth.

The milk of seven streakit cows
   It was their cost to keep,
They brought her daily, which she drank
   Before she went to sleep.

The spell on the girl could only be broken by kisses from her brother, the Child of Wynd, who was abroad. At last he returned, and despite the storms and the armed men that the wicked stepmother sent to hinder him, he did reach the Worm and give her the three disenchanting kisses. The stepmother was turned into a toad:

> Nor dwells a wight in Bamburghshire
> But swears the story's true,
> And they all run to Spindleston,
> The rock and cave to view.

This rock, which is said to be that to which the hero tethered his horse, can still be seen, but the Worm's Cave has been destroyed in the course of quarrying. At one time in the nineteenth century, a trough was pointed out to sightseers as being that from which the Worm drank its daily ration of milk; writing in the 1860's, William Henderson noted that local girls were frightened of meeting a venomous toad which was believed to haunt the beach near Bamburgh Castle, thinking that it would magically ruin their beauty.

## The Local Landowner as Hero

The process by which a widespread motif like dragon-slaying becomes attached to a particular place and takes root as one of its traditions will almost always involve the choice of a local hero as well as a local topographical setting. True, there are some cases where an anonymous knight will do, as at Churchstanton in Somerset, Sexhow in Yorkshire, Longwitton in Northumberland (see pages 75, 98–9) and in one version of the story from Lyminster in Sussex. In this last instance, however, one can see how the popular imagination seeks to forge local links for the hero; no name is given him, nor any details beyond the plain statement that he was a knight, yet at the end of the story it is said that in reward for his valour he married the daughter of the king of Sussex, settled in Lyminster, died there, and was buried under a particular stone in the churchyard. Moreover, at the time when this version of the tale was recorded (1886), there were people living in the district who claimed descent from this long-ago hero, though the collector, most regrettably, gives no information as to who they were.

It is far more common to find a named hero, and frequently the name given is that of some important landowning family of the aristocracy or upper class that had been long established in the district. Examples of such heroes are: the Seigneur de Hambye (Jersey); Sir Thomas Venables (Moston, Cheshire); Sir John Lambton, Sir John Conyers of Sockburn, and the founder of the Pollards of Bishop Aukland (all in County Durham); Sir Maurice Berkeley (Bisterne, Hampshire); one of the Garston(e)s of Mordiford (Herefordshire); one of the Wyvills at Slingsby and one of the Latimers at Well (both in Yorkshire); Sir Piers Shonks at Brent Pelham (Hertfordshire); Sir Hugh Barde or Bardolph at Castle Carlton (Lincolnshire); and one of the Somervilles at Linton (Roxburgh). In addition, there are Peter Loschy and Scaw, Yorkshire heroes at Nunnington and Handale Priory respectively, who are locally believed to have been knights who held land in the district, but who are more likely to be only fictional personages with names derived from hills and woods in the area where their stories are told. The same is probably true of a certain 'Grimesditch of Grimesditch' in Cheshire.

Several of these tales either state or very strongly imply that it was as a result of the hero's bravery in killing the dragon that his family was ennobled, or first received certain specified estates, or (if already ennobled) acquired additional land and privileges, which quite often included the right to have a dragon as crest to the family coat of arms. The most clear-cut cases of association between dragon-slaying and land-tenure, attested not only by a traditional story but by a ceremonial custom, are from County Durham.

The first concerns the Manor of Sockburn, near Darlington, which was held by the Conyers family. The condition of their tenure was that whenever a new Bishop was installed at Durham the lord of the Sockburn Manor must go to meet him at his first entry into the county, and standing upon Croft Bridge over the River Tees must there show him a certain falchion which was an heirloom in the Conyers family, saying:

MY LORD BISHOP – I here present you with the falchion wherewith the champion Conyers slew the worm, dragon or fiery flying serpent, which destroyed man, woman and child; in memory whereof the King then reigning gave him the Manor of Sockburn to hold by this tenure, that upon the first entrance of every Bishop into the country this falchion should be presented.[8]

The Bishop would then take the falchion in his hand, and immediately returning it would wish the lord of Sockburn health and long enjoyment of the manor. This ceremony is claimed to date from the time of Bishop Hugh Pudsey, that is to say from the reign of Richard I; it is certainly mentioned in connexion with the death of Sir John Conyers in 1396, and was also known to William Camden when he wrote *Britannia* in 1586. It was performed for the last time in April 1826 by the steward of Sir Edward Blackett, who held Sockburn at that date, on the occasion of the entry of Dr Van Mildert, the last Prince-Bishop of Durham, into the diocese. After the status of the see had been changed by the Palatinate Act, this ceremony was allowed to lapse; the falchion itself was deposited in Durham Cathedral Treasury, where it may still be seen. Other material objects which were connected with this tradition can be seen in Sockburn church, namely a stained glass window on which the falchion is shown, and a tomb on which both a falchion and a dragon are carved, and which local people sometimes allege to be that of the original dragon-slaying Conyers himself. This, however, cannot be the case if the hero really did live in Richard I's time, for the tomb can be dated to about 1310 or 1320; it must be that of some later member of the family, and the carvings upon it are simply derived from the family coat of arms, the crest of which was a dragon transpierced by a falchion.

The second tradition from this area is very similar. It concerns a piece of land called Pollard's Dene, formerly held by the Pollard family at Bishop Auckland, and here too the condition of tenure was to present a falchion to the newly appointed Bishop as he first entered his diocese; the earliest record of the ceremony is in 1399. The creature allegedly slain by the founder of the family is known either as the Pollard Brawn or as the Pollard Worm, according to whether it is being described as a huge wild boar or as a dragon. The latter version goes back at least to 1660, though the former is perhaps the more usual nowadays. As at Sockburn, there was a set speech at the presentation; as recorded in 1772 (when the weapon was being presented by a tenant, not by the Lord of the Manor himself) it ran:

> MY LORD! – In behalf of myself, as well as several other tenants of Pollard land, I do humbly present your lordship with this falchion, at your first coming here, wherewith, as tradition goeth, Pollard slew of old a great and venomous serpent, which did much harm to man and beast.[9]

Local storytellers have enriched the tale with many details. The Worm (or boar) is said to have lived in an oak wood – an appropriate haunt for a boar, and also no doubt a pun on the name Bishop Auckland. In reward for his prowess, Pollard was told he could have as much land as he could ride round while the Bishop was at dinner. This is a variation upon a condition found in several tales about the origins of estates or of tracts of common land, the condition usually being such that its fulfilment seems impossible or at least unlikely to bring much result (e.g. as much land as a woman can crawl round in one night). In this case the difficulty was solved by an impudent trick – Pollard simply rode once round the Bishop's castle, and would not give up his claim to it except in exchange for a very substantial estate. This tale, like the preceding one, had its material 'proofs' – the falchion used in the tenure ceremony (now unfortunately lost), and the family coat of arms, which in this case consisted of an arm brandishing a falchion.

These two tales can be classified as examples of what anthropologists call 'charter myths', i.e. tales which set out to explain the process by which a particular social institution (in these cases, ownership of an estate) first came into existence, and thereby to justify its continuation. There are several other local legends about dragon-slaying which, though lacking the clinching evidence of a tenure ceremony, are also probably charter myths; each serves to justify a local family's rank and landowning status by saying these were a reward bestowed on the founder (or an early member) because of his courage in killing a dragon. At Linton, for instance, the hero is named John Somerville in one version (the other simply calls him Laird of Laristone), and it is said that after his exploit, which allegedly took place in 1174, he was knighted, given the post of Royal Falconer, and created first Baron of Linton. The Somervilles, who were Barons of Linton, bore a dragon as their crest, and there is a carving in Linton church which shows a man with a falcon on his arm engaged in combat with a dragon.[10] According to some writers, there used to be a tablet by this carving which read:

> The Wode [i.e. crazy] Laird of Laristone
> Slew the Worm of Wormistone
> And won au Linton parochine [i.e. parish].

Again, in one of the accounts of how the dragon of Bisterne (Hampshire) was slain by a member of the Berkeley family, we read:

> One of the most celebrated of medieval dragon stories is connected with the manor of Bisterne . . . The whole of the surrounding country was for a long time terrified by a particularly dreadful dragon. He was eventually slain, however, by one Sir Macdonie de Berkeley in what is still known as the Dragon Field . . . The dragon figures in the Berkeley arms, and there is actually a deed in existence, temp. Edw. IV, which conferred knighthood on brave Berkeley and gave him permission to wear the dragon as his badge.[11]

There is a carving of a dragon's head over the entrance to Bisterne Park, which doubtless helped to keep the story going; the details of the slaying will be further discussed in the next chapter. A North Yorkshire tale explains the dragon on the arms of the Latimers by claiming that their ancestor slew a dragon which was terrorising the inhabitants of Well.[12]

Similarly at Castle Carlton (Lincolnshire) the story of the one-eyed dragon with the wart on his leg (page 42) ends in a knighthood and a royal grant of privileges being bestowed on the hero. The story was known in the sixteenth century, for William Camden included a reference to it in his *Britannia* in 1586:

> Sir Hugh Bardolfe . . . lived there in the time of Henry I . . . It is said in a very old court roll that in the first year that Sir Hugh was lord of the place 'ther reigned at a toune called Wormesgay a dragon in a lane in a field that venomed men and bestes with his aire; Sir Hugh on a

weddings day did fyght with thys dragon and slew him, and toke his
heade, and beare it to the kynge and gave it hym, and the kynge for
slaying of the dragon put to hys name this word *dolfe*, and did call him
afterwards *Bardolfe*; for it was before Sir Hugh *Barde*; and the kynge
gave hym in his armes then a dragon in sygne.'[13]

A modern version of the same story, written in 1926, adds many
flourishes of romantic high style, and also some further details of Sir
Hugh's rewards:

> And to him was granted the right to take a horn of salt from every salt
> cart passing through his domain, and to give permission to all sheriffs,
> bailifs and justices to arrest persons within the parish – nor could
> anyone be arrested without such permission – and the Mayor of Castle
> Carlton only was bidden to go every year to the toll court at Louth to
> demand freedom from all tolls for the tenants of Sir Hugh Bardolphe
> and his descendants for ever . . . While to this day is the memory of the
> brave knight cherished all round the hills of Carlton even to the
> outskirts of Louth, the ancient privileges granted by King Henry the
> First having been from those days faithfully observed.

When we turn to Sir John Lambton, the slayer of the famous Lambton
Worm and an ancestor of the Earls of Durham, we find that he was not the
actual founder of the family, but belonged to a subsequent generation.
Robert Surtees, in his *Antiquities of the County Palatine of Durham* (1820),
pointed out that this is exceptional among legends of this type:

> Like the *preux chevalier* of romance, the *homo propositus* of the name
> goes forth to slay wolf, bear or wyvern, and if on his return he does not
> marry the king's daughter, he at least receives broad lands and
> revenues for his guerdon. To this class belong the Worm of Sockburn,
> the Brawn of Pollard's Dene . . . But the Lambtons were a family of
> good and valorous repute long before the date of their family legend
> (which only ascends to the fifteenth century), and it does not appear
> that the hero reaped anything by his adventure, except the honour of
> achievement, and a very singular curse upon his descendants to the
> ninth generation.[14]

Nor is there any dragon or weapon in the Lambton arms, so on this
count, too, the Lambton legend differs from those so far discussed.
Perhaps – though this is no more than guesswork – there may be
significance in the fact that the particular Sir John Lambton who plays the
role of hero in the family legend is identified as one who belonged to the
religious order of the Knights of St John at Rhodes; he was serving in the

order at the time when his elder brother died, in 1442. About 100 years previously, the Grand Master of that order had been a certain Deodat (or Dieudonné) de Gozon, who held the office from 1346 to 1353; and this Deodat became the hero of a famous and colourful legend which alleged that he had once slain a dragon at Malpasso in Rhodes. This legend is known to have been circulating by 1521. One is tempted to think that it was already current when Sir John Lambton was in Rhodes in the 1440s, that he brought the story back to England with him, and that in due course his descendants, remembering his chivalrous career, thought it appropriate to ascribe a similar adventure to him. But such speculation cannot be proved, and quite different factors, now unguessable, might have first inspired people to think of Sir John Lambton as a dragon-slayer.

There are certain other cases where it looks as though the connection between dragon-slaying and a grant of land and privileges did at one time provide the main point of a local legend, but was later obscured, possibly because the family claiming descent from the hero had died out or left the district, with the result that the legend now survives with an altered tone and emphasis. Something of this sort seems to have happened at Brent Pelham in Hertfordshire, where there is a well-known tale about a dragon-slaying knight called Sir Piers Shonks. A family named Shank did hold property in this parish in the fourteenth century, including a manor-house known as Shonkes, and one man of the family, Peter Shank, was also granted another manor in the parish of Barkway by Richard FitzAlan, Earl of Arundel. Presumably this Peter is the same man as the 'Piers' of the local legends, of which there are two that concern us here. One says that Piers Shonks[15] was a giant who worsted a rival at Barkway, while the other, which is more frequently found, says that he slew a dragon. The theme of ownership of land is dimly reflected in the first, while the second has developed along quite different lines, and the stress is on Piers' death, his tomb, and his outwitting of the Devil (pages 93–4).

There is also reason to think that a connection with a landowning family was the key to a version, now barely recoverable, of the dragon story at Mordiford. Here, as many writers inform us, the focal point of the legend was a large painting of a wyvern which was to be seen for many years on the exterior wall of the church; according to a local historian, a Mr Broome, who described it in 1670, it was at that time accompanied by an inscription (since lost) which ran:

> This is the true Effigy of that strange
> Prodigious monster which our woods did range.
> In Eastwood it by Garston's hand was slain,
> A truth which old mythologists maintain.[16]

When J. Dacres Devlin was compiling his booklet on the Mordiford dragon in 1848, he found that nobody could remember who Garston had been, and that the versions then current all agreed in having an anonymous criminal as the hero (see page 68). He himself was inclined to think that 'Garston' was simply the name of this criminal, though he did also point out that there had been a family of that name living in Mordiford in the seventeenth and eighteenth centuries, some of whose activities were recorded in parish documents. Since these Garstons had been donors of various charitable gifts and doles to the parish, one can safely assume that their social status was not that of a common criminal; when it further appears, from heraldic books of reference, that there is a family of Garstons whose crest is a wyvern, the matter seems clinched. The original Mordiford dragon must have been two-legged, i.e. a wyvern, the original hero must have been a Garston, not a criminal, and the original function of the legend must have been the same as at Sockburn, Bishop Auckland, Bisterne and Castle Carlton: the glorification of the local landowners and the explanation of their arms and status. Only in later generations, with the death or departure of the Garstons, was the link broken and the story 'democratised'.

Such a change need involve only a slight shift in emphasis. If the hero had land, wealth, title or privileges after his deed, what had he been before it? The greater the contrast, the greater the dramatic impact of the tale. Thus at Deerhurst in Gloucestershire, according to Sir Robert Atkyns' history of that county written in 1712, an estate on Walton Hill was once offered by the king to anyone who could rid the area of 'a serpent of prodigious bigness' which was preying on cattle and poisoning people with its breath.[17] The man who accomplished the task and won the land was a mere labourer called John Smith. When Atkyns wrote, there was still a family named Smith holding the estate, and a connection of theirs, a Mr Lane, still kept the axe with which the original John Smith had done the deed. As will be seen in the next chapter, John Smith's mode of dragon-slaying was efficient but not chivalrous; despite the estate he won and the landowning family claiming descent from him, the story is more concerned with the earlier, rougher aspects of his career.

## The Village Heroes

In many cases, the storytellers are completely 'democratic,' and show no interest at all in honours and estates, in crests and heirlooms. Instead, the hero is presented as a typical sturdy working man – not a despised 'male Cinderella' (except in the one instance, the Orkney hero Assipattle), but a farmer, ploughman, shepherd, blacksmith, woodcutter, young farm labourer, sailor, soldier, or an anonymous brave man or boy. If he is given a name, it is a suitably plebeian one, but more often he is left nameless. Rewards are rarely mentioned; if they are, they are more often in money than in land, let alone titles. Sometimes, as at Bures in Suffolk and Henham in Essex, there is no individual hero, and the dragon is said to have been slaughtered or driven off by a concerted attack by all the village men, armed with stones, farm implements, or simple weapons. There is a description of such a battle in a Suffolk chronicle, the event being alleged to have occurred in 1405:

> Close to the town of Bures, near Sudbury, there has lately appeared, to the great hurt of the countryside, a dragon, vast in body, with a crested head, teeth like a saw, and a tail extending to an enormous length. Having slaughtered the shepherd of a flock, it devoured many sheep. There came forth in order to shoot at him with arrows the workmen of the lord on whose estate he had concealed himself, being Sir Richard de Waldegrave, Knight; but the dragon's body, although struck by the archers, remained unhurt, for the arrows bounced off his back as if it were iron or hard rock. Those arrows that fell upon the spine of his back gave out as they struck it a ringing or tinkling sound, just as if they had hit a brazen plate, and then flew away off by reason of the hide of this great beast being impenetrable. Thereupon, in order to destroy him, all the country people around were summoned. But when the dragon saw that he was again about to be assailed with arrows, he fled into a marsh or mere and there hid himself among the long reeds, and was no more seen.[18]

A story with a working-class hero may coexist in the same village with one where the hero is a knight or landowner. This must have been so in Mordiford during the transitional period before the Garstons were forgotten, and is still the case at Lyminster (Sussex). At Aller in Somerset, we find a mixed type of legend. The hero's name is given as John Aller – the same as that of the village – and he is sometimes said to be an ordinary local man, sometimes a knight; a spear said to be his has been preserved, but a farmer's unromantic harrow has also somehow become mixed up with the story, and in one version at least he needs the help of farm labourers to finish the job, although he is here called a knight:

> This poison-breathing monster, which had the shape of a great flying serpent and was protected by an armour of scales, lived in a den on the south side of the Round Hill above Aller. It descended to devastate the villages in the marshy valley, and wherever it flew the crops and trees were poisoned. Milkmaids fled at the first hiss of its wing-beat; and a score of pails had their contents drunk in a few minutes. People lived in

dread of a horrible death for themselves, their children, and their cattle. At last a knight called John of Aller, or the Lord of Aller, came boldly to their rescue. He plastered his body with pitch and put on a mask so that the dragon's breath could not harm him; he armed himself with a long spear specially fashioned for this exploit, journeyed to the dragon's den, and attacked it while it slept. After a fierce fight in the darkness, he killed it. Seeing two or three baby dragons in the den, he went home to fetch several of his labourers to stop up the hole with the spikes of an iron harrow . . . some who related the legend declare that 'The Dragon of Aller was slain by a harrow'. In the north wall of the chancel of Aller church . . . there lies the defaced effigy of a knight, with his dagger suspended by two cords from a richly ornamented baldric. He, they say, is John of Aller who killed the dragon, and the spear he used still exists. At one time it was kept in the belfry of Aller church, but now . . . [it is at Low Ham church.] It is a kind of dart nine feet long, made of light wood, its shaft curiously painted in a band-pattern of brown, green and yellow, with rings of black between.[19]

At Cnoc-na-Cnoimh in Sutherland, the hero is 'a rough and ready farmer from the Kyle of Sutherland, Hector Gunn by name', and though we are told at the end that King William the Lion 'rewarded Hector Gunn with gifts of land and money', no specific estate is mentioned, so the motif does not carry as much weight as in the English stories discussed earlier; probably it is no more than a conventional rounding-off of the story.[20] Similarly in the story from Dalry in Kirkudbright, we are told that the Lord of Galloway offered a reward for the killing of the serpent, but whether in land or money is not said; presumably the blacksmith who killed it then received the reward, but this is not made a point of importance in the tale.[21] Other examples of working-class heroes are Martin of Strathmartin (see page 38), the woodcutter of Shervage Wood and the 'bold man' of Kingston St Mary (both in Shropshire), Charles the Skipper of Ben Vair, a Welsh boy at Llandeilo Graban and another at Penmynydd, the soldier at Newcastle Emlyn, Jim Puttock and Jim Pulk at Lyminster (Sussex), and the henpecked tailor Billy Biter at Filey (Yorkshire).

The most extreme example of a low-status hero is the malefactor at Mordiford – an anonymous criminal under sentence of death, who is said to have volunteered to fight the dragon as an alternative to execution.[22] This disreputable personage was very popular with nineteenth-century storytellers at Mordiford, who described his exploit in several different versions. Some said he tracked the monster to its den in the woods, caught it sleeping, hacked it to pieces with his sword and tore out its tongue as proof that he had fulfilled his task; for this he was granted his life and freedom. Others, more numerous, spoke of 'the battle of the barrel'. According to this version, the criminal hid in a cider barrel at the junction of the rivers Lugg and Wye, where the dragon was in the habit of coming to drink, poked the muzzle of a gun through the bunghole of the barrel, and shot him dead. Or else, so others said, the barrel he hid in was bristling with knife blades and steel hooks which wounded the dragon horribly as he lashed himself against it, smashing the wood to pieces; the hidden hero jumped out and gave the dragon his death blow, but with his last breath the dragon poisoned him, and so both fell dead together. The same tragic fate overtakes the hero even in the versions where he stays inside the barrel and shoots from there, for the deadly breath seeps in through the bunghole, so that he never lives to enjoy the freedom he had earned.

### The Victorious Hero Slain

Similar bad luck befalls several heroes. We have already met the unfortunate Jim Pulk, whose celebratory drink was his undoing (page 51). The first recorded version of the story at Aller (Somerset), which was current in 1885, also ends in death:

> Many years ago a fiery flying dragon lived at Curry Rivell. At certain times it used to fly across the marsh to Aller, and destroy the crops and all it came near with its fiery breath. At last one John Aller, a brave and valiant man who lived at Aller, vowed that he would kill it. He lay in wait, and when next the dragon flew across to Aller Hill he attacked it, and after a fierce struggle slew it and cut off its head. Then its fiery blood ran out and scorched up all the grass around, and from that day to this grass has never grown on that spot. John Aller was so burned by the dragon's breath that he died almost at the same moment as the dragon. The people took up his body, buried it in the church, and called the village after him.[23]

The statement by this collector that John Aller was buried in Aller church can be linked up with that from the more recent version quoted earlier (page 68) about an effigy in that church which is said to represent the dragon-slayer; if a funerary monument becomes associated with a legend, the legend itself is very likely to take on a funereal tone.

It is not only heroes from among the common people who die these tragic deaths; several of the knightly heroes too are said to have died in the hour of victory, either from wounds or from the horror of what they had endured. Thus at Bisterne there is a tragic version as an alternative to the cheerful 'charter myth' version already quoted on page 63–4, and it is in fact the former which is the more widely known:

A tale concerning a dragon . . . is told in Hampshire. Covered in scales and belching fire, this dragon terrorized the village of Bisterne. Every day the creature descended from its lair on Burley Beacon to demand a pail of milk as its sustenance. But to the consternation of the neighbourhood, the dragon's diet was not restricted to milk – it also craved the flesh of both cattle and men. Eventually the villagers hired a famous knight, Sir Maurice Berkeley, to destroy the dragon. To protect himself against its fiery breath the champion plastered his body with bird-lime sprinkled with broken glass. Sir Maurice then took his dogs and confronted the formidable creature in Dragon Fields. In the fierce battle that followed the dogs perished, and though the knight succeeded in killing the dragon, he came from the field a broken man, and died soon afterwards without ever speaking of the struggle.[24]

At Brent Pelham in Hertfordshire, there is a similar divergence between various versions of the tale of Piers Shonks, whose alleged tomb is a focal point for the story told there (see pages 93–4). Writing in 1700, the local historian Sir Henry Chauncy said that Piers had died of his wounds immediately after the combat, whereas others say that it was only many years later that his death and burial occurred.

There is however no doubt about the pathetic fate of Sir Peter Loschy at Nunnington in Yorkshire. He had pitted himself against a dragon which was not only poisonous but also had the capacity to heal its wounds and to reunite severed portions of its body, simply by rolling on the ground. To overcome this problem, he had trained his dog to snatch up each segment as it was lopped off, and carry it to a hill a mile or so away. The plan worked perfectly, but the outcome was disastrous:

> No sooner was the terrible fight over than the dog, wagging his tail, ran up to his master. 'Well done, well done,' said Peter Loschy, patting his faithful ally on the head. As he did so the dog licked his face. On its tongue was some of the poison from the dragon's body, and instantly the knight fell dead in the very moment of victory, his dog afterwards dying of a broken heart.[25]

Once again, there is an effigy to go with the tale. In Nunnington church is the tomb of a certain knight, Walter de Teyes, with an effigy of him lying with his feet on a small lion; locally, this is said to represent Sir Peter Loschy and his dog. Not far away, at Slingsby, another church effigy shows a cross-legged knight with a dog,[26] and in 1619 a legend almost identical to the Nunnington and Bisterne ones was recorded there: the effigy was said to be that of a member of a local family, the Wyvills, who had perished with his dog shortly after killing a huge serpent, over a mile in length. We may also compare the story of the shepherd and his dog at Kellington, Yorkshire, with its associated tombstone (page 92).

The taste for tragedy takes another form in a story from the Channel Isles, from Five Oaks in Jersey. This tells how the Seigneur de Hambye valiantly slew a dragon, only to meet his death through the treachery of his own squire, who had watched the fight and murdered him while he was exhausted and off his guard.[27] The squire then claimed that it was he himself who had killed the dragon, and demanded the right to marry the Seigneur's widow as his reward; later his nightmares revealed the truth to her and thus his villainy was unmasked. This plot is a borrowing from a widespread fairytale, best known nowadays in the version printed by the Grimm brothers, where it is called 'The Two Brothers'. In the fairytale world, of course, where all evil can be magically undone, the dead hero is actually resuscitated by his faithful animals and makes a last-minute reappearance to prevent the princess marrying the false claimant, whom he unmasks by producing the dragon's tongue.

Another dramatic theme beloved of storytellers is the inescapable curse, and there are two dragon legends which exploit it. One is the well-known story of Sir John Lambton and his Worm, which normally (though not invariably) includes the following episode: In order to find a way of killing the Worm, Sir John consults a witch, who demands as her fee the life of the first creature he would meet after his victory; when this turns out to be his own father, he breaks his promise to her, and thus incurs a curse that for nine generations no Lord of Lambton Castle would die in his bed.[28] The ninth and last victim of the curse is said to have been Sir Henry Lambton, MP, who died in his carriage in 1761, though the curse is still sometimes recalled when misfortunes (not necessarily deaths) befall members of the Lambton family.

The second dragon-tale with a curse in it comes from Penmynedd on Anglesey.[29] Here the story goes that a family of local landowners, hearing a prophecy that a certain dragon in the neighbourhood would cause the death of their only son, sent the young man abroad for safety and offered a reward to anybody who could kill the monster for them. A clever local boy contrived to do so by a trick and was duly rewarded, and the corpse of the dead dragon was triumphantly displayed. The heir came home, viewed the corpse, which was by now a mere skeleton, and contemptuously kicked its skull; at once one of its sharp, venomous fangs gashed his foot, and so he died, as had been inescapably prophesied. Tales with plots of this type are not uncommon, for the inevitability of fate is a theme which for centuries has fascinated storytellers; here the theme is neatly grafted on to the basic dragon-slaying plot, in order to enhance still further its dramatic impact.

It is clear from this survey that British dragon-slayers do not conform to one single stereotype, though they can be grouped into certain definable categories: saints; heroes of medieval poems; past members of families of the nobility and gentry, usually but not always the founder; knights who remain nameless or are given fictional names; men, named or unnamed, who are the typical representatives of the ordinary community of rural workers; co-operating groups of villagers; and one criminal. Their fates are as diverse as their personalities. Some obtain a precisely defined reward in social status, ownership of land, and privileges of a legal sort; others get a vague, romantic reward reminiscent of fairytales (marriage to a king's daughter); others are offered a money reward; several die dramatically in the hour of victory; many, especially among the working-class heroes, simply slay their dragon, for this in itself is achievement enough. How this achievement is accomplished must be the theme of the next chapter.

# CHAPTER FOUR

## *The Tactics of Draconicide*

Those who set out to tell of a dragon-slaying, whether they are medieval preachers, epic poets, the transmitters of local oral stories, or the writers of children's books, find themselves facing a variation of the hoary old problem of the irresistible force and the immovable object. The dragon has to be truly terrible; the more fearsome his attributes, the more invulnerable he seems, the greater will be the dramatic impact of the story. On the other hand, the hero has to win. How can this be managed? On the solution of this puzzle depends much of the artistic effect created by the teller.

For the writers of medieval saints' legends there was, in a sense, no problem. The power of Almighty God was with the saint, whose radiant faith could summon up all its infinite resources; compared with this, Satan was helpless, and a mere flesh-and-blood dragon held no terrors at all. With thorough-going logic, icons of the Greek and Russian tradition frequently show a small, helpless-looking dragon being speared or trampled underfoot by a tall, imperturbable saint; the concept may outrage a Westerner's instinct for fair play, and is certainly lacking in the drama of conflict, but such considerations would be quite meaningless to the artist in comparison with the spiritual truth being conveyed. The writers of the saints' legends, being able to unfold their tale in stages rather than in a single visual image, were able to get the best of both worlds; they could describe as fully as they pleased the hideousness of the dragon, the damage he did, the terror which everyone felt at his coming, and then contrast this with the monster's sudden complete capitulation as the saint's holiness took effect on him. The outcome is easily foreseen, and the actual means used (combat, prayer, a crucifix displayed, the touch of holy water or of a sacred vestment) do not offer much chance of variety or surprise. The impact of such a story must have lain in the fact that it was fully believed by both teller and hearers; the point was not primarily excitement, curiosity or suspense, but awed admiration at the saint's unshakeable faith. And where faith is the guiding force, precise ways and means matter very little.

## Heroic Combats

In folktales with upper-class knightly heroes, it is surprising to observe how cursorily the actual combat (as opposed to the preliminary description of the dragon) is often handled. We are given a general indication that there was a long, fierce struggle, in which the knight relied on the customary weapons of his class, but few details, if any, are supplied. For example, we are told little or nothing about the actual course of the battles fought by St Leonard in Sussex, St George at Brinsop and at Uffington, Garston at Mordiford, Fulk Fitzwarren in Somerset, Sir Thomas Venables at Moston, the Seigneur de Hambye in Jersey, Scaw of Handale Priory, Wyvill of Slingsby, the anonymous knights of Sexhow, Churchstanton and Lyminster, Piers Shonks of Brent Pelham, or the founders of the Conyers and Pollard families. They must all be assumed to be straightforward chivalrous fights between man and monster, but in the surviving versions, at any rate, very little is done to convey the difficulties and dangers of the encounter, which are simply taken for granted.

There are two striking exceptions to this observation, but it is significant that both come from comparatively recent books whose authors have a marked liking for 'writing up' their material to suit a romantic taste. One is the tale of the dragon with the vulnerable wart, at Castle Carlton in Lincolnshire, as told in Christopher Marlowe's *Legends of the Fenland People* (1926). The stylistic contrast with William Camden's sixteenth-century version already quoted (page 63–4) shows how much elaboration Marlowe has lavished on the traditional story:

> Then did Sir Hugh cry to the Saints, and to Saint Bartholomew and Saint Guthlac in particular, promising to heap up riches upon the altar at Crowland if he might prove victorious that day. And he saw the blazing eye in the dragon's forehead fixed balefully upon him, and said: 'Thinkest thou to destroy me, O mine enemy? Now I challenge thee, and may St Guthlac defend me.'
>
> And at that the monster spread his wings and flew with the swiftness of the wind to seize the knight, as he stood at bay with his sword in his hand.
>
> Suddenly the clouds opened and a drenching downpour of rain came between the knight and his enemy, and a black darkness overshadowed him. And a voice came from the darkness, saying: 'Look for the bright light from heaven which shall blind the dragon – in the instant that light shines strike hard or thou shalt perish.'
>
> Whereupon there sounded a mighty thunderclap and a vivid flash illuminated earth and sky. And silhouetted against the darkness was the perfect outline of the monster, with the triple brass guard protecting his

thigh, standing out in bold relief. And on the instant Sir Hugh struck with all his strength so that his sword clave the brass guard in the middle and penetrated the wart and flesh beneath. Then did the dragon howl so that the noise was heard full twelve miles off, and opened his mouth and rushed upon the knight to devour him.

But again came the cloud and the sound of thunder so that he paused affrighted. And Sir Hugh stood awaiting the last onslaught, for he knew that his sword had opened the wart and that the monster must die. So the dragon wandered in the midst of the darkness seeking his enemy and breathing fire and brimstone. But the wound began to throb and he knew his last moments had come. So he stretched himself out on the earth, and the cloud vanished, and Sir Hugh saw him stiff and senseless on the beach. Then did the knight advance and with one stroke cut off that baleful head, so that it rolled well-nigh into the sea.[1]

The other instance, less deliberately archaic in style but equally detailed, is the account of the Dragon of Longwitton (Northumberland) in F. Grice's *Folk Tales of the North Country*, 1944.[2] This dragon is the one who so jealously guards the healing wells (page 39), and it has in addition the gift of making itself invisible at will. The hero obtains a magic ointment which enables him to see the dragon at all times, and confidently sallies forth to the attack; however, in the course of two whole days of ferocious fighting, he discovers that the dragon's wounds heal with miraculous speed, and its strength never diminishes. Close observation reveals the reason – it is keeping its tail dipped in the magic well. On the third day, therefore, the knight deliberately feigns retreat in order to lure it away from the well, and then contrives to place himself between it and the water; his strokes now take effect, and the combat soon ends in victory. Here, too, the modern author has allowed himself some elaboration; the version of the same story recorded early in the nineteenth century, which has Guy of Warwick as the hero, is more briefly told, though the main events are the same.

The versions of the Castle Carlton and Longwitton tales by Marlowe and Grice both have a markedly literary flavour, and it is indeed only in literature, in Spenser's *Faerie Queene*, that one can find a fully thought-out, detailed, visualised, blow-by-blow account of how a duel between an armed knight on horseback and a flying, fire-breathing dragon with claws and a spiked tail might be expected to unfold. In particular, Spenser makes good use of the dragon's power of flight. Early in the combat, the dragon snatches up the Red Cross Knight, horse and all, and attempts to fly off with them in his claws; but the weight is too much for him and he drops them, like a hawk that has swooped on a prey too big for it. The knight then slashes one wing from below, after which the dragon is grounded during the rest of the three days' fight. Neither the earlier romances about Fulk or Bevis, nor the later folktales, equal Spenser's precision in this matter.

The contrast with the folktales raises a curious problem. Quite a large number of local dragons are initially spoken of as fliers when the damage they do in the neighbourhood is being described, but (with the one exception, in the modern romanticised literary rendering of the Castle Carlton story) the power of flight is totally ignored once the hero and the monster are face to face. Why should this be? It is not that local storytellers lack the imagination to devise ways of destroying or outwitting even the most redoubtable monster; as will be shown below, they had a formidable armoury of tricks in their repertoire, and could certainly have thought up ways of disposing of a flying beast – arrows, spears, nets, catapults, traps and birdlime are all possibilities, yet none has been made use of. One can only assume that the explanation lies in the extraordinary conservatism of traditional storytellers. Wings, however common they may be in heraldry and in church art, are not after all essential to the basic concept of the Worm or *draco*, the huge earth-bound or water-dwelling snake, and it is to this ancient concept that the storytellers almost unanimously return when reaching the climax of their narrative.

## Tricks and Traps

If the heroic combats by a knight armed with normal weapons usually lack precision and detail in the folk legends, the very opposite is true of the second and more extensive class of dragon slayings, those where some unconventional device is used against the monster. Here the storytellers obviously revel in the variety and ingenuity of the tricks they ascribe to their heroes (some of which are decidedly not fair play), and especially in the cunning way in which they use simple means to obtain unexpected results, or turn aspects of the dragon's own behaviour into means of overcoming him. Not surprisingly, the division between the 'heroic' combats and the 'trick' combats corresponds fairly closely to that noticed in the previous chapter between upper-class and lower-class heroes. The only plebeians to adopt the heroic method of a straight fight are Martin at Strathmartin and John Aller at Aller, and in both cases there are dubious points which make categorisation difficult. Martin uses a club, not generally considered a noble weapon; and in the case of John Aller there are variations in the story affecting both his social status, his choice of armour and weapon, and his helpers. Conversely, heroes of gentle birth do not generally resort to eccentric weapons and deceitful tricks, though there are some striking exceptions, notably at Linton and Bisterne, not to mention the undignified antics recounted in 'The Dragon of Wantley' (Appendix A, pages 146–50).

To start with the simplest methods. One may block up the dragon's burrow, either while he is inside it, as John Aller's workmen did with their harrow in order to prevent the young dragonets from emerging; or while he is out of it, so as to force him to go elsewhere, as at Ludham in Norfolk:

A fearsome winged dragon once terrified the people of Ludham in Norfolk by appearing in the village every night, so that no one dared to venture abroad after dark. Each morning, when the monster had returned to its lair, the villagers filled up the entrance with bricks and stones, but these failed to prevent the dragon from making his nightly excursions.

One afternoon the inhabitants were horrified to see the beast issuing from its burrow. When it had gone some distance away, a courageous man placed a single round stone in front of the lair, completely filling it up. The dragon, after basking in the warm sunshine, returned home, but finding it impossible to move the stone, made its way, lashing its tail with fury and bellowing loudly, over the fields towards the Bishop's Palace and along the causeway to the ruined Abbey of St Benet, where it passed under the great archway and vanished in the vault beneath. After a time its former lair was filled in and the people of Ludham saw no more of the dragon.[3]

Another simple way of getting rid of young dragonets is to burn their lair, if this should happen to be in a cornstack, as was the case at the foot of Ben Vair, near Ballachulish:

When the farmer discovered them in his stack, he at once set fire to it, hoping to destroy the brood. The shrieking of the young dragons was borne on the wind up to Corrie Lia, and the mother leapt down to their assistance. In spite of her efforts, however, they were burned to death; and when she saw this she lay down in her grief on a flat rock near the shore, and lashed at the rock with her tail until she killed herself. The rock upon which Ben Vair House now stands is still known as Leac-na-Beithreach (The Dragon Rock).[4]

In Somerset, there is an amusing anecdote about a woodman and a dragon that lived in Shervage Wood:

It was a long dragon, 'one of the sort they call a worm', and it devoured every living thing within reach. Consequently the local woodman was unable to go to the wood and cut the faggots on which his living depended. At last, however, starvation drove him to work at a time when the dragon seemed to have gone elsewhere in search of prey, and during the morning he cut wood unmolested, seeing and hearing nothing of the terror. At noon he sat on a fallen log half buried in fern to eat his 'nummit' (noon-meat), and as he sat, the log heaved under him. Whereupon in desperation he leaped up, and crying 'So thee do movey, do'ee? Take that then!', he struck his axe into the beast, and fled. But what became of the dragon afterwards no man knows, for it was never seen again.[5]

It is also easy, though hardly sporting, to kill the creature while it is sleeping, especially after a heavy meal; this occurs in two versions of the Mordiford story, one being that already referred to in the previous chapter where it is said that the criminal caught the sleeping dragon in his lair, and the other an alternative version in which the dragon gorged himself on a drowned ox after a flood, fell asleep, and was hacked to death by a combined attack of all the men of Mordiford, armed with scythes, axes and so forth. Much the same thing happened at Deerhurst (Gloucestershire), where the labourer called John Smith put out a large quantity of milk for the dragon, who swallowed it eagerly and then 'lay down in the sun with his scales ruffled up. Seeing him in that situation Smith advanced, and, striking between the scales with his axe, took off his head.'

Another method, which is elementary in its principles but devastating in its effect, was used in Somerset, at Kingston St Mary:

> There were a terrible dragon to Kingston St Mary, breathed out viery vlames he did, an' cooked his meat to a turn, looky zee. Well, no one couldn't get near to kill'n vor vear of bein' roasted so brown as a partridge. Now, there were a bold veller as had a good head on him, and he climbed lane by Ivyton where there was a gurt rock in those days. 'Tis a steep hill, look, and rock was right on brow, so he gave a shout to dragon. Well then, dragon he do look up and zees'n. Then he opens his gurt mouth to roar vlames, and the veller gives the rock a shove off. It rolled straight down hill into dragon's mouth and choked'n dead. Yes, it did.[6]

## Hiding Places and Protective Coverings

If one intends to fight one's dragon at close quarters, there are obvious advantages in concealing oneself in some way so as to take him by surprise. The criminal at Mordiford hid inside a cider barrel at the spot where the creature usually came to the river to drink, and for the same reason More of More Hall lay in wait for his quarry, the Dragon of Wantley, inside a well (See Appendix A, pages 148–50). The oddest hiding-place – or protective covering? – was that chosen by Sir Macdonie de Berkeley in one version of the Bisterne story:

Sir Macdonie combined courage with craft, like so many old-time heroes, and went out against his dragon armed only with his sword and a jug of milk, and a glass case in attendance. Arrived in the dragon's neighbourhood, he put the milk into cans, and stepped into the glass case. He waited till the creature came and tasted the milk, and killed him as he lapped. A singularly tame end, one would think, for such a dreadful dragon.[7]

Not only tame, but a bit confused too, perhaps; the fondness dragons feel for milk is something which has been mentioned several times already, but what function the glass case is supposed to have fulfilled remains mysterious. It may possibly be a device borrowed from those once numerous stories about a man who destroyed cockatrices by going up and down the country 'in glass', as Topsell tells us, so that their baleful gaze should be reflected onto themselves: if so, its occurrence at Bisterne could be due to influence from the story of the Wherwell cockatrice (above, pages 46–7), since that village is in the same county. Another story which looks as if it is a variation on the same theme is the one at Penmynedd in Anglesey.[8] There a boy dug a pit, put a highly polished brass pan in it, waited until the dragon was exhausted through fighting its own reflection, and then killed it easily. A cockatrice is the subject of the following ingenious Welsh tale:

Castle Gwys, near Haverfordwest, is now known as Wiston. Centuries ago there were several claimants to this estate. In the days of old a serpent lived in a hole in Wiston Bank, not far from the castle. This serpent possessed innumerable eyes, and it was impossible for anybody to gaze at the creature without the latter seeing him.

It was agreed by the kindred of the family that the person who could gaze on the reptile 'without the same serpent or cockatrice seeing him' should be the lawful heir of the estate. Accordingly, several of the claimants tried every imaginable way to accomplish this object, but without success. One of them formed a plan, but kept the secret to himself until the time came when the others had given up the attempt. Then he took a barrel to the top of the hill, secured himself in it, and allowed it to roll down the bank past the exact spot where the serpent placed itself. As the man passed the spot where the serpent was stationed he peeped through the bunghole and said: 'Ha, ha! Bold cockatrice, – I can see you, but you cannot see me!' In this way the claimant became owner of the Wiston estates.[9]

It is pleasing, for once in a way, to read a tale in which the hero need only outwit the creature, not slaughter it, in order to get his reward.

It is understandable that a would-be dragon-slayer requires special armour. Even Beowulf ordered a new shield to be made for the occasion; it was entirely of iron, since a wooden shield could never resist the dragon's fiery breath for long, and it was unusually large, so that in the later stages of the fight both Beowulf and his nephew were able to shelter behind it. The protective coverings donned by folktale heroes can be a good deal odder. Notable examples are the pitch with which John Aller plastered his body and the 'birdlime sprinkled with powdered glass' which Sir Maurice Berkeley used in the same way (pages 68, 70). It is not clear from the existing versions of these stories what exactly the purpose of this grotesquely undignified procedure is supposed to have been; was it meant to render the hero so nauseous that the dragon would not swallow him or bite him? Or did it form a waterproof covering which drops of venom or splashes of poisonous blood could not penetrate? Or was it possibly some form of disguise? Whatever it may have meant, it is not confined to English folktales; in the medieval Icelandic saga about Ragnar Lodbrok ('Shaggy-Breeks'), we read that that hero boiled his clothes in pitch and then rolled in sand before doing battle with a dragon. This, it has been suggested, was an actual procedure used in the early Middle Ages by warriors who could not afford proper mailcoats.

Be that as it may, the favourite device in British folktales, which recurs again and again in various forms, is the suit of armour (or other object) studded with spear-heads, razorblades, knives, spikes, or sharpened hooks.[10] And there is no doubt how this is meant to work – the dragon, who is envisaged as having the instincts of a python or a boa constrictor, coils round his enemy and attempts to crush him, but in doing so he inflicts mortal injuries on himself. To use such armour is the advice given to Sir John Lambton, in what is probably the best known among British dragon legends (see Appendix A):

> He was told . . . that he must have his best suit of mail studded with spear blades, and take his stand on the rock in the middle of the river . . . The more closely he was pressed by the worm, the more deadly were the wounds inflicted by his coat of spear blades, until the river ran with a crimson gore of blood.

The tone here is perfectly serious, as it also is in the story of the luckless Sir Peter Loschy of Nunnington (page 70), who also had recourse to spiked armour as well as to the help of his dog. But the same device is used with comical effect in 'The Dragon of Wantley', where the spiked armour worn by the hero, More of More Hall, makes him look like a ludicrous monster himself:

*Cover of an anymous pamphlet giving the legend of the
Lambton Worm, 1875*

> Had you but seen him in this dress,
>   How fierce he looked and how big,
> You would have thought him for to be
>   Some Egyptian porcupig.
> He frightened all – cats, dogs and all,
>   Each cow, each horse, and each hog;
> For fear did they flee, for they thought him to be
>   Some strange, outlandish hedgehog.

The combat in this case ends when a kick from More's spiked steel boot pierces the dragon's only vulnerable spot, which turns out to be its arsehole – at least, that is how it is put in the original verses printed as a broadside ballad in 1685 (see Appendix A, page 150), though later prose paraphrases have glossed over this and several other unedifyingly coarse details in this farcical tale.

The most elaborate and devastating of these suits of armour is one mentioned in a Scottish story collected by Andrew Lang from oral tradition in Kirkudbright, and published by him in 1885. It was made by a blacksmith of Dalry, in order to destroy a huge white snake which lay twined round Mote Hill, and its special feature was that the spikes upon it were retractable. Wearing this armour, the blacksmith allowed himself to be swallowed by the snake, and suddenly caused the hidden spikes to shoot out all over him; he next began to roll about violently inside the snake's belly, and thus tore it apart from within. By the time he had forced his way out, the snake was quite dead, and for three days the Water of Ken ran red with its blood.

Both the idea of being swallowed alive by a monster and the idea of spiked armour have parallels outside Britain, as will be discussed in Chapter 8. The spikes also raise an interesting possibility: their popularity may have been inspired by a dramatic spectacle in the natural world, namely a fight between a viper and a hedgehog. Concerning this, the naturalists Ramona and Desmond Morris write:

> The hedgehog has long been known to do battle with the viper. It is reported to bite the viper's tail, curl up, let the enraged snake dash its head onto its sharp spines, unroll again, bite the damaged viper once more, roll up, and so on. Eventually the snake, blinded and bleeding from striking at an invincible sea of spikes, is easily killed and eaten.
>
> Something like this has undoubtedly been witnessed, but the sequence has, in the re-telling, got a little out of step. A hedgehog is forty times as resistant to viper venom as a guineapig, but even so would hardly risk deliberately antagonizing the reptile, and is certainly not

cunning enough to calculate a complicated ruse for luring the serpent to its death. If a hedgehog on the hunt met a snake, it might well take a bite at it. If the meal resisted violently, the hedgehog would immediately react with its generalized fear response by erecting its spines and rolling up. If the snake struck it would damage itself. The hedgehog, on cautiously unrolling, might find a juicy meal. If the meal was not quite cooked and lashed out again, the hedgehog would be alarmed once more and would roll up again. There is a subtle difference between this description and the usual 'outwitting the dragon' way of telling the story.[11]

If a man in spiked armour looks like 'a strange, outlandish hedgehog', so too, even more so, does a barrel with spikes sticking out all over it.[12] At Mordiford, as noted already (pages 68–9) the barrel used by the criminal as his hiding place is sometimes said to have been bristling with knife blades and steel points, while in Argyll a more elaborate version of the same device was used against a female dragon on Ben Vair:

> No one dared to attack the dragon, and no one could think of a plan for her destruction, till Tearlach Sgiobair (Charles the Skipper) came to Ben Vair. He anchored his boat some distance out from the site of the present pier, and built a bridge of empty barrels between the vessel and the shore. The casks were lashed together with ropes, and bristled with spikes. When the bridge was made, he lit a fire on board the boat and placed pieces of meat on the embers.
>
> When the odour of burning flesh reached Corrie Lia [the dragon's lair], the dragon jumped down in a series of mighty leaps to the shore, and from there tried to make her way out over the barrels to the boat. The spikes, however, pierced her scaly hide and tore her flesh so badly that she was nearly dead before she reached the other end of the bridge.
>
> Charles the Skipper had meanwhile rowed his boat further out, so that a gap was left between it and the last barrel of the bridge. The dragon had not sufficient strength to leap to the deck of the boat, nor to return the way she had come; so she died of her wounds where she was, at the end of the bridge.

In Denbighshire, at Llanrhaeadr-ym-Mochnant, there is a standing stone known as the Red Pillar (Post Coch) or the Pillar of the Viper (Post-y-Wiber), because legend asserts that the people of the village once draped it in red cloth and studded it with concealed spikes, in order that a flying dragon should batter itself to death against it.[13] It would seem that Welsh dragons, like bulls, were easily provoked by the colour red; there was one at Llandeilo Graban who was also infuriated by it, according to a story current in the early years of this century. The monster used to settle on top of the church tower every night to sleep, until a ploughboy thought up a way of killing it at no risk to himself:

> He made a dummy man out of a large log of oak, and, aided by the local blacksmith, armed it with numerous iron hooks, powerful, keen and barbed. Then he dressed the dummy in red and fixed it firmly on top of the tower. At dawn the following day the dragon first saw his daring bedfellow, and dealt him a violent blow with his tail, which was badly torn by the hooks. Infuriated by the pain, he attacked the dummy with tooth, claw, wing and tail, and finally coiled himself round his wooden foe and bled to death.[14]

Wyverns, the two-legged variety of dragon, were also readily susceptible to red objects. There once was a fire-breathing wyvern that lived in the ruins of the castle at Newcastle Emlyn (Carmarthen), and a certain soldier set out to shoot it.[15] In order to distract its attention he flung a piece of red flannel into the river; the wyvern hurled itself furiously at the flannel, which gave the soldier the chance to shoot it through the only vulnerable spot in its shell-like hide, which was its navel. That a reptile should possess a navel is not the least remarkable item in the story! Perhaps, as at Wantley, what is really meant is a serpent's vent; if so, the theme of the 'one vulnerable spot' ought to be regarded as another example of attempted realism on the part of the storytellers, rather than as fairytale fantasy. If one has imagined a reptilian monster covered all over with impenetrable scales, then the vent and the open mouth are indeed the only two places available for a successful attack.

### The Fatal Food

A different type of plot turns on the hero's cleverness in taking tactical advantage of the dragon's greed and his tendency to swallow things indiscriminately. Milk can serve as a bait to distract him or as a satisfying meal to send him to sleep, as we have already seen in stories from Bisterne and Deerhurst (page 78). It is also possible to put poison into his food, as Jim Pulk did with the pie at Lyminster (page 51), beheading him afterwards to make assurance doubly sure. But the most entertaining tricks in this category arise when some perfectly normal everyday food proves to be a dragon's undoing, because of his greed and because of his unfamiliarity with its possible pitfalls.

One tale of this type originated in Yorkshire, though it has been preserved through a Somerset narrator and collector, and it tells how the Dragon of Filey met his downfall when he encountered a certain Billy Biter and his parkin – a parkin being a kind of sticky treacle-flavoured gingerbread much enjoyed in Yorkshire. Billy, the hero of the tale, is a henpecked tailor whose cottage stands at the edge of a gulley in which a dragon lives, and one night he falls over the edge while carrying a parkin which a kind neighbour has given him:

> 'Twas no wonder that misty moisty night he stepped right over the edge of the Dragon's gulley, and down he went arsey-varsey almost down his gullet too. He landed on his load, which were softer than all the oven-hot rock down there, and up against a girt red light that blinked.
>
> 'That be my eye you be poking your faggot in,' say Dragon. 'Let's have a proper look at what I'm to dine on.'
>
> Poor Billy's knees chattered and he dropped his wedge of parkin afore Dragon's nose – out come a girt hot tongue and golloped it . . . But the parkin wouldn't gollop; it stuck to Dragon's teeth, and he found it so welcome as flowers in May.
>
> 'What do ee call this?' he say through the sticky chumble.
>
> 'P–p–parkin,' say Billy, still atwitter and all adrench with cold sweat. For all that, his load were beginning to scorch gentle.
>
> 'Then go back and bring me some more,' say Dragon, sneezing out a crumb as were tickling his gullet. That sneeze fair blew Billy clean out of the gulley . . . [16]

It is in fact Billy's shrewish and drunken wife who insists on baking the next parkin, a round one, which she drops; it rolls to the edge of the gulley, and she in turn falls into the depths, where the dragon swallows her:

> 'Twasn't a very tasty morsel,' he say, and then the girt round parkin, what had been a-spinning and wig-wagging on the edge above, plumps down right before his nose. 'Cor!' say Dragon, and he bit into it that hearty that he couldn't say no more, and he never did, on account of his teeth were that stuck he could only snort.
>
> When the folk seed what come of it they all ran for sledgehammers and pitchforks and axes and such, but how to get down into the gulley they couldn't tell. Dragon he settled it for 'en nicely. He took off away down to the sea to wash the girt round parkin from between his teeth, where it were clinging so loving as an ivy-bine. Well, the folk followed, and they was just in time to see Dragon ker-vlop right down in deep water and stuck his head under, then they run and give his nose arf-dozen whistlepoops as stopped his breath, and run back to safety, and afore Dragon come to there were a girt oncome of waves, and he drowned then and there.
>
> Charley say Dragon's bones formed into a long stretch of rock folk up there call Filey Brigg, but I ain't never heard on 'en.

It is implied in this story that the fortunate outcome, which delivers Billy from his wife at the same time as it rids the district of the dragon, has all been planned, or at any rate foreseen, by the kindly neighbour who baked the first of the two parkins, being herself something of a white witch; Billy himself, however, is merely a lucky fool. On the other hand, Jim Puttock, the hero of the fullest of the four versions of the story from Lyminster (see Appendix A), knew exactly what he was up to when he cooked a vast and indigestible pudding for the Knucker, who devoured it gleefully, but suffered hideous after-effects:

> Afore long they hears 'en rolling about, and roaring and bellering fit to bust himself. And as he rolls, he chucks up gert clods, big as houses, and trees and stones and all sorts, he did lash about so with his tail. But that Jim Puttock, he weren't afraid, not he. He took a gallon or so with his dinner, and goos off to have a look at 'en.
>
> When he sees 'en coming, ole Knucker roars out: 'Don't you dare bring me no more o'that there pudden, young man!'
>
> 'Why?' says Jim, 'What's matter?'
>
> 'Collywobbles,' says Dragon. 'Do sit so heavy on me I can't stand up, nohows in de worruld.'
>
> 'Shouldn't bolt it so,' says Jim. 'But never mind, I got a pill here, soon cure that.'
>
> 'Where?' says Knucker.
>
> 'Here,' says Jim. And he ups with an axe he'd held behind his back, and cuts off his head.[17]

For the full appreciation of this tale, the reader needs to know that a 'Sussex Pudding' was a crude concoction of flour and water which was the staple food of farm labourers in the days of rural poverty when even bread and cheese, let alone meat, was far too expensive for daily use. This 'pudden' was notoriously heavy and indigestible, especially if eaten cold, as it had to be by those who took their midday meal into the fields with them. The Revd W. D. Parish, a nineteenth-century student of Sussex dialect, alleged that it promoted chronic indigestion and finally undermined the constitution; whether or not he was right in this gloomy diagnosis of its effect on men, it certainly seems to have been quite devastating to dragons.

## The Smouldering Peat

Up in Scotland, an equally homely object is unexpectedly transformed into a powerful weapon, namely a lump of burning peat. A Sutherland farmer named Hector Gunn used one to destroy the Worm of Cnoc-na-Cnoimh (Worm's Hill) in Glen Cassley, after he had discovered in the course of a first encounter that the hot, poisonous fumes of its breath were more than he could bear:

> When he had recovered somewhat from his faintness, he borrowed a seven-ell-long spear, and asked the astonished villagers if they had any pitch. They said that they had, and he ordered them to boil some of it in a pot. He then went onto the moor and cut a great divot of peat. He thrust the end of the long spear through the peat, and dipped it into the boiling pitch. With this strange weapon in his hand, he mounted his horse once more and rode towards Cnoc-na-Cnoimh. The country people followed at a distance, wondering. As soon as Hector Gunn came near the monster, and it opened its mouth to suck him in with its poisonous breath, he held out the spear with the reeking peat at the end, and the wind blew the fumes right into the worm's face. So strange and pungent was the smoke that the creature was almost suffocated, and drew in its breath, and wound itself tighter round the hill in its agony. Hector rode nearer and nearer, until he was on a level with the monster, then in one quick movement he thrust the burning peat down its throat and held it there till the fearsome creature died.[18]

One of the heroes of nobler birth, the John Somerville of Linton who became the first Baron Linton (see page 63), used exactly the same tactics against his adversary, the Worm of Wormistone, except that he constructed his weapon a little more elaborately than Hector Gunn did. It was not a plain lance, but one on the point of which he had fixed a wheel, and it was to the wheel that the peat was tied; no doubt the purpose of this was to prevent the peat being driven back up the shaft. Also the scalding hot mixture was even more nauseous, for it included boiling resin and brimstone as well as pitch. It is probably no mere coincidence that there is a wheel on the Somerville coat of arms.

Finally, in a fantastic variation upon the same theme, comes the Orkney tale of Assipattle and the Stoor Worm. The Worm was so vast, mile upon mile of it stretched out along the bed of the sea, that Assipattle's plan was to let himself be swallowed down its gullet in a small boat when the monster yawned at dawn. In the boat was a pail with a smouldering peat in it. As the sea water rushed down the Worm's throat Assipattle's boat was drawn in with it, and when at last it came aground somewhere deep in the monster's belly he jumped out and ran at full speed through the phosphorescent inner tunnels, till he found the Stoor Worm's liver:

> He pulled out a muckle knife and cut a hole in the liver. Then he took the peat out of the pail and pushed it into the hole, blowing for all he was worth to make it burst into flame. He thought the fire would never

take, and had almost given up hope, when there was a tremendous blaze and the liver began to burn and sputter like a Jonsmas bonfire. When he was sure that the whole liver would soon be burning, Assipattle ran back to his boat. He ran even faster than he had done before, and he reached it just in time, for the burning liver made the Stoor Worm so ill that he retched and retched. A flood of water from the stomach caught the boat and carried it up to the monster's throat, and out of his mouth, and right to the shore, where it landed high and dry.[19]

There can be no doubt that stories such as these, combining suspense, humour, and economy of means, appeal to present-day hearers as much as ever they did to our great-grandfathers, and to their ancestors before them. Even though we can no longer think of dragons as real, even though the religious symbolism so important in medieval times is being fast forgotten; even though an interest in the founders of ancient families may be only a minority taste; still, in spite of everything, one is both thrilled and amused to learn a new method by which the irresistible force of human ingenuity overcomes that immovable object, a dragon.

# CHAPTER FIVE

# 'You Can See it There Still'

In quoting the stories of Jim Puttock, Hector Gunn and Assipattle in the previous chapter, I stopped at the points where each had triumphantly killed his respective adversary. This, however, is not how the stories actually conclude. The Sussex one adds this final piece of information about the hero:

> If you goos through that liddle gate there into the churchyard, you'll see his grave. By the porch, left-hand side, in the corner like, between the porch and the wall of the church.

The Scottish story ends by pointing to the landscape:

> And to this day men may go to Cnoc-na-Cnoimh and see traces of this old story in the spiral undulations said to have been made on the hillside by the worm, as its coils tightened in its death throes.

And the Orkney one, which ends in true fairytale style with the hero's wedding to the princess whose life he has saved, first tells us this:

> The Stoor Worm twisted and turned in torment. He flung his head up to the sky, and every time it fell the whole world shook and groaned. With each fall, teeth dropped out of the vile spewing mouth. The first lot became the Orkney Islands; the next lot became the Shetland Islands; and last of all, when the Stoor Worm was nearly dead, the Faroe Islands fell with an almighty splash into the sea. In the end the monster coiled himself tightly together in a huge mass. Old folk say that the far country of Iceland is the dead body of the Stoor Worm, with the liver still blazing beneath its burning mountains.

## The Local Setting

Such endings are as significant for a local legend as 'they lived happily ever after' is for a fairytale, and they fulfil several different functions. Artistically, they bring an exciting story to a quiet conclusion, rounding it off firmly and harmoniously. But even more important is the way in which they direct the hearer's attention back onto his own material environment, pointing to the well-known landscape, the church, the monuments seen every day, and so clinching the relationship between the astounding events which have just been described and the familiar world in which, so it is alleged, they took place. Nothing could more clearly sum up the difference between a local legend and the never-never land of the fairytale, with its 'Once upon a time' opening and its happy but unreal ending, than the way in which these specific local allusions are satisfactory when they appear in the former, but seem out of place in the latter. ('Assipattle and the Mester Stoor Worm', which is nine-tenths fairytale in tone, characteristically escapes anticlimax by choosing its topographical details on a very grand scale – whole islands, rather than a mere grave or a single hill.) Thirdly, the local allusions constitute a claim upon the hearer's belief: how could anyone feel doubts about the dragon's reality when he can climb its hill, see the bare patches burned by its blood, or visit the hero's tomb? A nineteenth-century countryman in Hertfordshire is recorded to have said, in connection with the story of Piers Shonks which will be given below (pages 93–4):

> It's one of the rummiest stories I ever heard, like, that 'ere story of old Piercy Shonkey, and if I hadn't seen the place in the wall with my own eyes I wouldn't believe nothing about it.[1]

Even when a story happens to be being used as a pokerfaced leg-pull, as practised by locals on 'foreigners', or by older boys on younger ones, an appeal to concrete evidence will serve the purposes of the leg-puller just as well as those of the convinced believer.

Unfortunately, since it is only in fairly recent years that folktale collectors have fully appreciated the importance of recording storytellers absolutely verbatim, and have had conveniently portable equipment with which to do so, most British dragon tales exist only in summaries and paraphrases, having passed through a writer's recollections of what he has been told, probably by more than one informant. One cannot therefore safely assert that all oral narrators round off their tales with conclusions like those quoted above, but certainly the collectors and summarisers have included so many references to actual objects, place-names, and details of scenery that we can be sure that these allusions must have been very frequent features in the stories and in the comments and conversations surrounding the actual act of storytelling. Sometimes, indeed, a collector clearly states that this is what occurred. For example, Ruth Tongue, after telling the tale of the dragon of Kingston St Mary quoted in the last chapter, comments that her informants showed her the very spot from which the rock which the hero rolled down the hillside had been dislodged. The local farmer who told the Aller legend to a collector in 1885 pointed out a noticeably bare sandy patch on a hill as the site where the dragon was killed, and its blood stopped the grass from growing. When Bishop Percy published 'The Dragon of Wantley' in his *Reliques of English Poesy*, he gave in the footnotes to the later editions the following verbatim extract from a letter which an unnamed correspondent sent him about it in 1769:

> In Yorkshire, six miles above Rotherham, is a village called Wortley, the seat of the late Wortley Montague Esq. About a mile from this village is a lodge, named Warncliffe Lodge, but vulgarly called Wantley: here lies the scene of the song. I was there above forty years ago; and it being a wooded rocky place, my friend made me clamber over rocks and stones, not telling me to what end, until I came to a sort of cave; then asked my opinion of the place, and pointing to one end says, Here lay the dragon killed by More of More Hall; here lay his head; here lay his tail; and the stones we came over on the hill, are those he could not crack; and yon white house you see half a mile off, is More Hall. I had dined at the lodge, and knew that the man's [i.e. the lodge-keeper's] name was Matthew, who was a keeper to Mr Wortley, and, as he endeavoured to persuade me, was the same Matthew mentioned in the song; in the house is the picture of the dragon and More of More Hall; and near it a well, which, he says, is the well described in the ballad.[2]

Just as the tale-teller seized on topographical features, pictures, church monuments and so forth as evidence of the truth of the story, so too the historian and folklorist will attribute much importance to them, but for the opposite reason, seeing in them a stimulus for the first invention of the legend, a focal point for its development, and a memento which helps to preserve it through following generations.

## Tombstones

The part played by church monuments is particularly noteworthy, especially by tombs with effigies or heraldic devices (several of which have been mentioned already), and by tombs which had become mysterious because no one could remember whose they were. There are some good examples in Yorkshire. The first concerns a 'curious stone coffin' with an illegible inscription, which was found among the ruins of Handale Priory, near Lofthouse, and which contained an Elizabethan sword.[3] In the 1840s, a local informant maintained with great conviction that it had held the body of a youth named Scaw, who had won the hand of an earl's daughter, together with vast estates, by slaying a dragon in Scaw Wood. However, it appears that there has never been any family of this name in the district, so it probably was simply the name of the wood which, combining with the existence of the mysterious tomb, inspired a local story about an imaginary hero. There is another interesting tombstone legend at Kellington:

> In the churchyard at Kellington, near Pontefract, there is an old stone in a horizontal position, which may have been the cover of a stone coffin, or may have been monumental. Upon this is cut what appears to be in the middle a cross, and on the right side of it a man with clasped hands, at his feet a dog; while on the left of the cross are some indecipherable marks, which may have represented a serpent. There are other figures upon it, but too much worn away to be distinguished.
>
> The explanation given by legend of these figures is that 'once upon a time', in the dim and distant past, the dark and dank marshy woodlands then around Kellington harboured an enormous serpent, which wrought terrible destruction among the flocks of the surrounding shepherds. At length a shepherd named Armroyd, more daring than the rest, determined to do battle with the monster. By the aid of his shepherd's crook and his faithful dog, he prevailed and slew the enemy, but alas at the expense of his own life as well as the life of his dog. They perished together, and this stone, bearing the figures of them all – of the man, his dog, his shepherd's crook, and of the slain monster, is an enduring testimony to the facts of the story.
>
> A field in the neighbourhood, named Armroyd Close, is said to have been given to his descendants by his grateful neighbours, as a recognition of the service he had rendered. It has since passed from Armroyd's descendants to other owners.[4]

There is an interesting instance of misinterpretation here; the cross on the worn stone is taken to be a shepherd's crook and is woven into the story in that role, just as at Nunnington a lion at the feet of an effigy is taken to be the dog which plays a major part in the legend.

Similarly at Lyminster there is an anonymous medieval grave-slab which was formerly in the churchyard near the main entrance, but has now been moved to the interior of the church to save it from further weathering. It is mentioned as a 'proof' in every recorded version of the story of the Knucker, and though it cannot have been the first starting-point for the invention of the legend (the place name 'Knucker Hole' must be older), it has certainly helped to maintain it in memory through the ages. One oddity in this case is that the decoration on the stone only fits in well with one version of the tale, that where the hero is a knight. This decoration, which is almost worn away, originally consisted of a full-length cross superimposed on a background of oblique ribbing; it is interpreted as a sword laid across the ribs of the dead dragon. A sword, obviously, is only suited to a knightly hero; yet the storytellers who spoke of Jim Pulk with his scythe or Jim Puttock with his axe still maintained that this same gravestone was that of their hero, even though its decoration had nothing in common with the story as they told it [5]

A legend which owes a great deal to the physical appearance and situation of a tomb is that of Piers Shonks, at Brent Pelham in Hertforshire. In the church, there is an elaborately carved monument, probably dating from the thirteenth century, though it has been rather heavily restored; its marble cover shows the symbols of the four evangelists, an angel bearing a soul to heaven, and a large foliated cross, the foot of which is thrust into the jaws of a two-legged dragon. This tomb is set in a deep recess in the north wall of the nave, a position which has given the local story an ending unique among dragon-slaying legends:

> The lair of the Brent Pelham dragon was a cave under the roots of a great and ancient yew tree that once stood on the boundary of Great Pepsells and Little Pepsells fields. A terror to the neighbourhood, this dragon is said to have been a favourite of the Devil himself.
>
> One day, so the story goes, Piers Shonks, the lord of Pelham, who lived in the moated house the ruins of which are still known as 'Shonkes', said by some to be a giant, and by most a mighty hunter, set out to destroy the evil monster. In full armour, with sword and spear, Shonks was accompanied by an attendant and three favourite hounds, so swift of foot that they were thought to be winged. Shonks at length found the dragon, and after a terrible struggle thrust his spear down the monster's throat, giving him a mortal wound. The forces of evil, however, had not been overcome, for the Devil himself now appeared and cried vengeance upon Shonks for the killing of his minion. The Devil vowed to have Shonks' body and soul, when he died, were he buried within Pelham church, or outside it. Nothing daunted, Shonks defied the Devil, saying that his soul was in the Lord's keeping, and that his body would rest where he himself chose. Years later, when Shonks lay dying, he called for his bow, and shot an arrow that struck the north wall of the nave of Pelham church. There Shonks' tomb was made, and there, as he had foretold, his body rests in peace beyond the Devil's reach: neither within Pelham church nor outside it.[6]

Burial 'neither inside the church nor out of it' is known elsewhere in British legends as a means of thwarting the Devil; for instance, the magician Jack o' Kent (a popular person in Herefordshire and Gwent) once struck a bargain with Satan by offering his own soul whether he were buried in a church or outside, and then cheated the Devil of his due by being buried in the thickness of a wall. The position of the Brent Pelham tomb has drawn this motif of cheating the Devil into the orbit of Piers Shonks's story; the carving upon it, showing an angel bearing a soul away, may have helped the process, and the cross thrust into the dragon's mouth which also appears on the tomb presumably determined the precise method whereby Piers dealt with the monster. As for the attendant and three hounds 'so swift they were thought to be winged', I suspect that – amazing as such a misunderstanding must seem – they were inspired by the symbols of the evangelists on the tomb, i.e. one winged man and three winged animals!

The tomb of Piers Shonks is also interesting because it supplies some evidence as to when the legend arose. It can be dated on stylistic grounds to the thirteenth century; it bears no inscription itself, but on the wall by it is a tablet inscribed in Latin and English:

> Tantum fama manet Cadmi sanctique Georgi
> Posthuma; tempus edax ossa sepulchra vorat.
> Hoc tamen in muro tutus, qui perdidit anguem,
> Invito positus Daemone, Shonkus erat.
>
> O PIERS SHONKS
> WHO DIED ANNO 1086
>
> Nothing of Cadmus or St George, those names
> Of great renown, survives them but their fames;
> Time was so sharp set as to make no Bones
> Of theirs, nor of their monumental Stones.
> But Shonks one serpent kills, t'other defies,
> And in this wall, as in a fortress, lies.

The Hertfordshire historian Nathaniel Salmon, writing in 1728, declared that these verses were written by the Revd Raphael Keen, who died in 1614 after having been Vicar of Brent Pelham for almost 76 years; they show knowledge not only of the dragon-slaying but also of the significance of the wall-burial *invito Daemone* whereby Piers 'defied t'other serpent', i.e. the Devil. Both these elements of the legend, therefore, must have come into existence before the mid-sixteenth century, the period of Keen's incumbency, though they cannot of course antedate the tomb itself, which is of the thirteenth. As the arch above the tomb and the brick base on which it rests seem to be of Tudor date, it is likely that Keen restored and embellished it. In addition, he must have known some tradition, now lost, which led him to assign the date 1086 for Piers' death – a date which is in fact far too early to suit the tomb, or to fit the fourteenth-century date of the Peter Shank with whom Piers is probably to be identified (see page 65). Considering these various dates, and bearing in mind that some lapse of time must be allowed for folk imagination to work upon the carvings of the tomb and the memories of the life of the real Peter Shank, it seems likeliest that the legend of Piers Shonks the Dragon-Slayer developed during the fifteenth century.

## The Mordiford Painting

Another influential monument whose history can be traced in some detail is the figure which could at one time be seen on the exterior west wall of the church at Mordiford. It is first mentioned by the antiquary John Aubrey in the course of the notes he gathered between 1656 and 1685 for his *Naturall Historie of Wiltshire*. He described it as a painting of a serpent with four pairs of wings, 'one of them added since my remembrance', and he evidently had had reason to observe that many people thought it the reliable record of a real creature, since he complained that this shows 'how apt the World is to be impos'd upon, even in things against Nature and against the Staticks'.[7] At roughly the same period (1670), a local historian copied some verses about the 'effigy' into his collection (see page 65), presumably in reference to the same wall-painting. In 1802 comes another allusion, in George Lipscombe's *Journey into South Wales*; he does not speak of multiple wings, but simply calls it a large green dragon with a red mouth and a forked tongue, and says it is on the east wall – an error, unless there were perhaps at this time two paintings on different walls. According to J. Dacres Devlin, there were several re-paintings of the figure (on the west wall) during the eighteenth and early-nineteenth centuries. Usually it was done in green, but sometimes in red; generally it had only two legs, which, technically, classes it as a wyvern rather than a dragon, and had its tail curling up sharply. In about 1800, it was redone as a green-and-gold lizard-like creature with four legs, two wings, and a long straight tail. Finally, and most regrettably, it was erased when repairs were done to the church in 1810–12, and it has never since been renewed.

In addition to this main representation of the Mordiford dragon, there seem to have been others; Devlin speaks of two fragments of stained glass still kept in the rectory in his time (1848). One showed an erect, winged, 'four-legged wyvern' with a curly tail, and the other a wingless dragon with a long straight tail. These presumably must have been remnants of stained glass windows from the church removed or broken in earlier times; it would be useful to know whether they had been of religious subjects or simply of heraldic devices, but Devlin gives no further information about them. Equally tantalising is a drawing done in about 1808 by C. Dingley and subsequently published in *History from Marble* (1867–8), which shows what, from the shading and shadows, is clearly meant to be a three-dimensional free-standing figure of a dragon, not a painting or a window. The editor of this work says of it: ' . . . a drawing of a dragon, having four pairs of wings and four pairs of feet. It has been conjectured that this dragon (to which Dingley has attached no description) was suggested by the legend of the dragon of Mordiford, if it was not actually a copy of the monster which was formerly exhibited on the exterior of that church at the west end.'

In the absence of any indication of scale or background, it is impossible to decide exactly what the drawing represents; a weathervane is one possibility, though there is no staff supporting it, and another is a portable figure for use in pageants or processions, as will be described in the next chapter. In any case, it is not even sure, from the editor's comment, whether the drawing has anything to do with Mordiford or not.

The wall painting itself, however, is very well attested from about 1660 till 1812, though it underwent so many re-paintings in the course of its career that it is impossible to tell what it originally looked like as regards colouring, number of wings and legs, and so forth. Both Devlin and the Herefordshire folklorist Mrs Leather argue that it must have been meant to be a wyvern, and point out that the living of Mordiford was at one time in the gift of the Priory of St Guthlac in Hereford, which had a wyvern in its arms. An alternative theory, I would suggest, is that it was the wyvern crest of the Garston family (see page 66), and that it was displayed on the church wall either as a memorial to some member of the family or as a tribute to their importance as benefactors of the parish. The pieces of stained glass might have come from memorial windows donated by the Garstons bearing heraldic allusions to their arms. The verse recorded in 1670 is one piece of evidence pointing emphatically to the Garstons rather than to the Priory as the likely object of these heraldic tributes. But whatever its origins, the stimulating impact of the painting on the imaginations of the villagers cannot be doubted – someone, sometime, had killed a dragon in Mordiford, and there to prove it was the picture, endorsed by the authority of the Church, and visibly present as a daily reminder through at least six generations, to be proudly explained to every child and every passing traveller.

## Miscellaneous Monuments and Mementos

Besides containing tombs with effigies or heraldic carvings, stained glass windows, and ancient carvings, and being surmounted by picturesque weathervanes, churches were also used as depositories for all sorts of intriguing objects – chests, weapons, pieces of armour, flags, old alms dishes, flagpoles, maypoles, wreaths, gloves, and even an iron cauldron, have all been recorded. Many more such curios, their origins forgotten, seem to have littered English country churches before the zeal of earnest and historically learned clergy in the nineteenth century swept them away in the course of church 'restoration'. The spear of John Aller is one example of this fascinating ecclesiastical bric-a-brac. When one also considers the wealth of medieval carvings, both in stone and wood, whose symbolic meanings and allusions to saints' legends became incomprehensible once Catholic teachings had been forgotten, and likewise the mysterious fragments of old wall-paintings which must have become partly visible from time to time as the whitewash applied by the Reformers peeled off, it is clear that the physical appearance of a village church in the seventeenth and eighteenth centuries must have been a most fruitful (though unintentional) stimulus for the growth of folk legends.

At Crowcombe in Somerset, for example, there is a bench-end carved with a two-headed dragon, the second head being on its belly. Locally, this is alleged to be a monster slain by a man from the village.[8] Again, there are carved dragons in the Somerset churches at St Decuman and Cleeve, which may be linked in tradition with the one St Carantoc tamed at nearby Carhampton (page 55). In Norwich, home of the famous Snap who will be discussed in the next chapter, there is a church that has a wall-painting of St George and the dragon. Deerhurst in Gloucestershire has in its church several large, ferocious stone animal heads of Anglo-Saxon date, one set over the outer door, two over inner doorways, another over a window, and two more at the chancel arch; local storytellers assert that one (or all) of them represent the Deerhurst Dragon. The St George tympanum at Brinsop inspired a legend, as we have already seen (page 53). So, probably, did the one at Linton, but here it is not certain what the carving originally meant; some authors describe it as a man in combat with two monsters, while others say the second 'monster' is meant to be the Lamb of God. If the latter is correct, then the composition was intended to show the Christian combating evil under the inspiration of Christ, an allusion to Revelation chapter 12, 'They overcame him by the blood of the Lamb.' It is typical of the way in which the old system of religious symbols was forgotten that such a carving, however worn away, could be taken to show a local laird choking a worm with a smouldering peat.

Though the church was one centre of village life, and its monuments and carvings were an inescapable part of everyone's experience, it was not the only place where such things could be seen. The family seat of a major landowner would be sure to display his coat of arms in various prominent places, for instance at the lodge gates or over the main entrance; his crest or the supporters of his arms could turn up in many different guises – on garden ornaments, on paintings or tapestries, on vehicles, on servants' liveries, on innumerable domestic objects. So if there was some traditional tale bound up with these arms, visual reminders of it would be extremely familiar throughout the neighbourhood. One example of this is at Bisterne Park (Hampshire), where one can see a carved dragon over the main entrance, this being an allusion to the arms of the Berkeleys; the house also has ornamental statues of two dogs on its terrace, which doubtless accounts for the two faithful hounds which helped Sir Maurice de Berkeley to slay his dragon.

Where the family rights of manorial tenure were bound up with a particular object, this object was of course preserved as a precious heirloom, and its existence served to maintain and endorse the legend. This, clearly, was the function of the Conyers falchion and the Pollard falchion and perhaps also, at one time, of the axe which the Smiths of Deerhurst kept until the eighteenth century. At Lambton Castle, neither coat of arms nor land tenure was involved, but various objects could be seen there which encouraged the legend to survive. There is a stone trough, said to be that from which the Worm lapped its daily ration of milk, a statue of the hero with spikes on the back of his armour, thrusting his sword into a dragon's mouth, and another statue of a woman, which some say represents the witch who advised him. At one time in the nineteenth century, a piece of some tough and horny substance was on display in the castle as a fragment of the dragon's hide.

This last item raises a curious point. It would seem a simple and obvious move for someone to produce faked remains of dragons, by using, say, ribs or vertebrae of whales, elephants' tusks, or, best of all, fossil skulls and bones of prehistoric creatures. Fakes were common enough in other areas of folk tradition, for instance narwhal tusks sold as unicorns' horns, stuffed compounds of fish and monkey exhibited as mermaids, a mammoth's shoulderblade at Coventry and a whale's rib at Warwick Castle, both alleged to come from the gigantic Dun Cow slain by Guy of Warwick. On the Continent, stuffed crocodiles or fossils were formerly on view as dead dragons at Aix, Marseilles, Lyons, Ragusa in Sicily and Brno in Czechoslovakia – the last indeed, a crocodile, can still be seen there. The fossil at Klagenfuhrt has already been mentioned (page 20); until recently, it could be seen there in the Town Hall. Yet in Britain there is very little trace of anything of this sort; the piece of hide at Lambton Castle is matched by only one similar relic, formerly at Stokesley, but now lost:[9]

> Sexhow is a small hamlet or township in the parish of Rudby, some four miles from the town of Stokesley in Cleveland. Upon a round knoll at this place a most pestilent dragon or worm took up its abode; whence it came or what its origin no one knew. So voracious was its appetite that it took the milk of nine cows daily to satisfy its cravings . . . Its breath was so strong as to be absolutely poisonous . . . At length the monster's

day of doom dawned; a knight clad in complete armour passed that way, whose name and country no one knew; and after a hard fight he slew the monster and left it dead upon the hill, and passed on his way. He came, he fought, he won, and then he went away. The inhabitants of Stokesley took the skin of the Worm and suspended it in a church over the pew belonging to the hamlet of Sexhow, where it long remained, a trophy to the knight's victory and their own deliverance from the terrible monster.

Stuffed crocodiles were at one time a fairly common sight in the shops of apothecaries, usually being hung from the ceiling as their trade-sign, and those might be alleged to be dragons, to impress the gullible. Writing in 1886, J. Larwood and J. C. Hotton recorded that 'such a stuffed crocodile is still to be seen in a pharmacy at Arundel in Sussex'. Was this apothecary trying to cash in on the popularity of the legend about the Knucker of Lyminster, which certainly had connexions with nearby Arundel? If so, he did not succeed in impressing local opinion, for no Sussex writer seems to mention his crocodile.

As for fossils, in the museum at Taunton (Somerset) is a skull of an ichthyosaurus which was found at Glastonbury in the nineteenth century. According to a recent folklore collection, a jocular story has grown up to the effect that it is the skull of a dragon called Blue Ben who lived inside Putsham Hill and got accidentally drowned at Kilve. However, this seems a fairly recent and quite frivolous flight of fancy. Nobody in modern times could have really believed that this fossil was once a dragon.

## Place-names

Another type of 'evidence' used by storytellers in pursuit of precision and verisimilitude is that provided by place-names. In one form, this consists of relating the hero's name to that of a piece of land well known in the locality: Sir Peter Loschy and Loschy Hill at Nunnington, Scaw and Scaw's Wood at Handale Priory, Armroyd and Armroyd's Close at Kellington (all three in Yorkshire), or Green and Green's Acres at Wherwell (Hampshire). If there is no independent evidence for the real existence of these heroes, the cautious student will conclude that they are invented personages, their names having been created by back-formation from existing place names which had had some quite different origin. Sometimes, as at Strathmartin (page 38), it is obvious that the whole story has been tailored to fit in with a series of village names; punning verses are a common feature of village humour, which has here left a particularly clear mark on the evolution of a dragon legend.

It is more difficult to assess the numerous cases where the evidence consists of a place-name containing the words Worm, Dragon, Drake, or their Welsh or Gaelic equivalents. Did the names cause the legend, or did the legend cause them? And consequently, is the date at which they are first recorded the latest or the earliest date at which the legend can be said to have begun? Is the place-name a corruption of something else, and if so how long would it have taken for the original meaning to be forgotten? For example, it is claimed locally that the fifteenth-century account of a dragon 'near Bures' (page 67) properly relates to a village called Wormingford, about two miles away from Bures on the Essex side of the River Stour; Wormingford is also the site of an oral dragon legend current nowadays (page 116). The fact that the village name contains the syllable 'Worm' must obviously have favoured it in this takeover of the Bures story and in the growth of a further tradition.[10] However, the oldest recorded form of the name is 'Withermundeford', and it passed through several other variations during the Middle Ages before settling down to the memorable and easily pronounced 'Worm-'. It is thus a very open question whether the dragon legend of the Stour Valley influenced the simplification of the place-name or vice versa, and at what period the influence was exerted.

These tangled problems are a challenge to local historians and to philologists, each case requiring separate and careful investigation. Yet in one sense their solution is not after all as important as one might suppose; the really vital role played by place-names, as by concrete objects, is to keep the story alive, to be a constant reminder of its existence and its relationship to the environment and the community. From a functional point of view, what matters is not so much whether a particular place-name originated the legend or was, on the contrary, derived from it, but that there should be people asking 'Why is that hill called Worm Hill, or that lane Serpent Lane?' and receiving the traditional story in reply.

# CHAPTER SIX

# Dragons in Plays and Pageants

The dragons we have so far considered have been products of the storyteller's art, existing only in the minds of the people who passed on tales about them; at the most, it might be claimed that some carving or painting commemorated their past existence. It is time to pass to more substantial dragons – not indeed of flesh and blood, but at least of wood and wickerwork, paint and canvas – the portable and often 'workable' effigies which were a fairly common feature in religious plays and processions of the late Middle Ages, and which survived, transferred to secular contexts, through the sixteenth century and into the seventeenth. Gradually they became rarer and rarer, but there remains one group of authentic representatives, the 'Snaps' of Norwich, whose ancestry can be traced back in unbroken line to 1408.

## The 'Snap-Dragons'

The Norwich 'Snaps' have recently been studied in detail by Richard Lane,[1] so it will be convenient to begin with a description of their appearance and mode of operation, although there were also other types of dragon figure. The 'Snaps' are so designed that they can be manipulated by one man only, who walks inside the figure, his head partly concealed by its wings, and his legs covered by a hanging canvas tube. The dragon's body is barrel-shaped, and balanced in a horizontal position; through it runs a stout horizontal pole, of which the front end bears a carved and painted wooden head, while the back end protrudes for several feet as a rigid tail, its weight counterbalancing that of the head. The framework of the body rests on the operator's shoulders as he stands inside it; it is strapped to him in such a way that his hands are free to manipulate the head, which can swing from side to side, nod up and down, and snap its lower jaw which works on a hinge and is reinforced by a loudly clacking metal plate. The junction of head and body is covered by a neck of fabric, painted to represent scales, and this fabric continues over the body; a pair of small wings (which in some Snaps were moveable) rises at the mid-point of the back, hiding the operator's face from spectators at the side; a canvas 'skirt' (sometimes painted with reptilian legs and feet) conceals as much as possible of the operator's legs. This mode of construction is like that of hobby-horses of the 'tourney' type (e.g. Hobnob of Salisbury), except that the latter are fastened at waist level, not balanced on the shoulders, so as to give the impression of a horse and rider. It goes without saying that a dragon would be carved and painted in such a way as to look as grotesque and alarming as possible, and it is not surprising to find the scholar John Florio, in 1611, alluding to 'a disguised or uglie picture to make children afraid, as wee say, a snap-dragon, a turke, a bug-beare.'

## The Festive Dragon

And yet, as will be seen, fear was by no means the chief reaction which dragon images evoked. To see them in a fair light, it is worth quoting a well-known passage in which an eye witness vividly describes the excitement at some sixteenth-century rural merrymaking in which a dragon was playing a minor part. The writer is Phillip Stubbes, a Puritan author whose *Anatomie of Abuses* (1583) was intended as a furious denunciation of the Popish survivals and appallingly frivolous customs which he saw all around him, and which he regarded as so many snares of Satan, leading straight to paganism, blasphemy, sexual licence, and the neglect of true religion. Yet such is the energy of his scorn that, paradoxically, he succeeds surprisingly well in conveying the infectious gaiety of the very things he so much detests. In this passage, he is describing some Midsummer festivities at which a Lord of Misrule presided, attended by Morris dancers, at an open-air fair with booths and feasting; the description does not apply to one particular place but is a general picture of what apparently could be seen at that time in any typical English village. He tells how the Lord of Misrule is chosen and crowned by 'all the wilde heads of the parishe', and how he in turn picks anything from twenty to a hundred 'lustie guttes like to hymself' to be his attendants:

> They bedecke themselves with scarfes, ribons and laces, hanged all over with golde rynges, precious stones, and other jewelles; this doen, they tye about either legge twentie or fourtie belles, with rich handkerchefes in their handes, and sometymes layed across over their shoulders and neckes, borrowed for the most parte of their prettie Mopsies and looving Bessies for bussynge them in the darke. Thus all thinges set in order, then have they their hobbie-horses, dragons, and other antiques [i.e. grotesque figures], together with their baudie pipers and thunderyng drommers, to strike up the Deville's daunce

withall: then marche these heathen companie towards the churche and churcheyarde, their pipers piping, drommers thonderyng, their stumpes dauncyng, their belles jynglyng, their hand-kerchefes swyngyng about their heades like madmen, their hobbie-horses and other monsters skyrmyshyng amongst the throng: and in this sorte they goe to the churche (though the minister bee at praier or preachying) dauncyng and swyngyng their hand-kerchefes over their heades in the churche, like devilles incarnate, with such a confused noise, that no man can heare his owne voice. Then the foolishe people, they looke, they stare, they laughe, they fleere, they mount upon formes and pewes, to see these goodly pageauntes solemnized in this sort. Then after this, aboute the churche they goe againe and againe, and so forthe into the churcheyarde, where they have commonly their sommer halles, their bowers, arbours and banquetting houses set up, wherein they feaste, banquet and daunce all that daie, and (peradventure) all that night too. And thus these terrestrial furies spend their Sabbaoth Daie![2]

The picture is a joyous one, full of life and gusto. It is also something of a jolt to one's preconceptions about dragons, since if they stand for danger, destructiveness, or even (in Christian art) the Devil, then what are they doing here, dancing merrily into church beside the Morris Men and the hobby-horses, and 'skyrmishyng amongst the throng'? And why is the crowd's reaction one of amusement and pleasure? Similarly at Norwich, Snap's latest biographer finds something paradoxical about the affection he inspired:

To modern generations these dragons might be somewhat of a mystery, but to those old enough to remember their appearances in the streets of Norwich in the early years of this century, there is a warm almost hereditary affection for them . . . . It seems strange at first sight that 'good master Snap' should have obtained such an esteemed position, especially when his mythological ancestors were symbols of evil. Our legends are rich with stories of dragons capturing fair maidens, and the noble knights who rode to their rescue. In the end it was the dragon who was vanquished – the triumph of good over evil. Yet Snap was a dragon who in his way vanquished the people of Norwich by winning a place in their hearts.[3]

Even a dragon of recent origins, without the centuries of tradition which Snap can boast of, evokes the same response of affectionate amusement from present-day crowds. At least one group of Morris dancers (the Chanctonbury Morris Men, in Sussex) is accompanied by a 'hobby-dragon' which mingles with the audience, to the delight of children who rush to feed coins into his snapping jaws. There is no doubt that to them he is the star of the show, and perhaps some adults feel the same.

## Medieval Religious Plays and Pageants

The history of dragons in English folk-drama and folk-pageants begins, as does so much else in this field, with the semi-theatrical aspects of medieval religion. For instance, in the late medieval cycles of Mystery Plays on themes drawn from the Old and New Testaments, which were presented as open-air dramatic pageants in several large towns, the 'Mouth Of Hell' was symbolised by the head of a huge dragon-like monster opening to engulf sinners, and emitting fire and smoke; this prop would be used in plays about Christ's Harrowing of Hell, and in those about the Last Judgement which brought the cycle to a spectacular close. Again, the actor representing the Serpent in the Garden of Eden must have had a reptilian costume, and if he also had wings to denote his Satanic nature, the effect would have been distinctly dragonish.

It is sometimes asserted that dragon-images were carried in the processions held at Rogation tide (i.e. the three days before Ascension Day) in pre-Reformation England. This was certainly done in many towns and villages in France, where in some places the dragon so used has survived to this day; writing in the 1860s the antiquarian Robert Chambers claimed (though without citing any evidence) that the same had once been done in England:

> In the ancient [Rogation] processions there was always carried the image of a dragon, the emblem of the infernal spirit . . . whose final defeat was attributed to the saint more particularly revered by the people of the diocese or parish. On the third day of the procession, the dragon was stoned, kicked, buffeted, and treated in a very ignomini-ous, if not indecent, manner. Thus every parish had its dragon as well as its saint, with a number of dragon localities – the dragon's rock, the dragon's well etc. – so named from being the spots where the dragon was deposited when the procession stopped for refreshments or prayers.[4]

Unfortunately, the considerable research into English folk-customs that has taken place during the last century does not support Chambers' assertion, since no specific documented example of this alleged use of dragon figures in this country has ever (so far as I know) been produced. Modern works of reference make no mention of it when describing old Rogation-tide ceremonies. It is possible that Chambers may have known of some isolated instance, and have rashly generalised on the basis of this and of the undoubtedly widespread French custom; possibly he was drawing on a remark made by William Hone in 1823 to the effect that Rogation dragons *might* have existed in England as well as France, and converted Hone's tentative hypothesis (which is more a question than an assertion) into a positive statement of his own. Or he may simply have been speculating, seeking an explanation for minor place-names like Dragon's Well, and for the fairly frequent mention of dragon images in old parish records. The latter, however, are more plausibly explained as connected with the plays and processions in honour of St George, the existence of which is well attested.

The cult of St George, which was certainly of great importance in the history of British dragons, grew ever more popular towards the end of the Middle Ages. Having first won acclaim as a soldiers' patron during the Crusades, George was enthusiastically adopted by orders of chivalry both in England and on the Continent. In 1348, Edward III founded St George's Chapel at Windsor, and the following year, during the siege of Calais, he added George's name to that of Edward the Confessor in his battle cry. From then on, George was officially regarded as the patron saint of England, and in 1415 his feast day, 23 April, was raised to the same status as Christmas Day, namely that of a major double feast, on which all labour was forbidden. There is ample evidence of plays and processions in which St George's exploits and martyrdom were celebrated, and in these a dragon naturally played a prominent part.

The best documented tradition is that of Norwich, where it is known that a religious St George's Guild was founded in 1389 'to the honour of St George and his feast', members being bound to celebrate this day by attending Mass. By 1408, the festivities had assumed a semi-dramatic form, as is known from the Guild's resolution in that year that 'the George shall go in procession and make conflict with the dragon'. A few years later, when an inventory was taken of the Guild's possessions, these included fine armour and weapons for the man impersonating George, and also 'a dragon' – which could mean either a statue of one, or perhaps already a mobile man-operated figure like the later Snaps. From the many descriptions of the Guild's procession in the fifteenth and sixteenth centuries, and the account books in which expenses relating to it were recorded, a detailed picture of the ceremony can be reconstructed. It took place, naturally, on St George's Day, April 23. As the Guild was not only a religious confraternity, but also an organisation with much importance in the civic life of Norwich, the procession included both religious and secular elements; some of those taking part wore monks' habits and carried sacred banners, crosses, and candles, but there were also the Mayor and Aldermen in their robes of office, and Guild members in their liveries.

The central figure was always St George, either represented by a statue (as in 1461) or, more usually, impersonated by a man who was paid from five to ten shillings for his pains. As Richard Lane writes:

> St George rode on horseback and wore armour of beaten silver, beneath which was a colourful toga made of expensive material and trimmed with fur. He carried a silver shield painted with the arms of the saint. His mount too wore armour, but in later processions the armour of both steed and saint was carried by attendants. The same costume was not worn every year – sometimes it was borrowed, or at other times new material was purchased. Account rolls for 1492 show that his gown was made from twelve yards of green satin costing £4. Another example comes from the 1537 roll when material of tawny and crimson velvet was bought from London. The horse was decorated in ribbons and laces with red velvet for the cheeks of the bridle.
>
> In the legend St George rescued a maiden, and she was eventually introduced into the procession under the name of St Margaret. The first mention of her is in 1532. Her horse was decorated like that of St George, and she wore a colourful costume adorned with a chain and jewels.
>
> With them was the Snapdragon, smoke and sparks belching from his fearsome mouth, his bat-like wings beating against his barrel-shaped body. He rushed from side to side, threatening the crowd, which revelled in his comic malevolence. The man who operated the dragon was paid less than the saint. In 1420 it was 4d; 1429 2s 4d; and in 1500 it was 12d . . . The procession ended at the Cathedral, where there was Mass in honour of St George. Snap, symbol of evil, was not allowed to enter the holy precincts, and had to remain outside seated on the 'dragon stone'.[5]

The identification of St Margaret with St George's maiden-in-distress is a surprising departure from the conventional biographies of both saints, but the explanation can be guessed. The clue lies in the fact that she, like George, was reputed to have been a dragon-slayer, though her method of slaying was purely spiritual, as befits the unwarlike nature of a female saint. Margaret of Antioch, whose feast falls on 20 July, was a purely fictitious person, but her legend was widely known. It was said of her that while in prison awaiting martyrdom, she prayed to be allowed to see her adversary the Devil in corporeal form; at once a huge dragon appeared, to her terror, but rallying her courage she held out a crucifix, which caused it to vanish. Or, in another version of her story, she was actually swallowed by the monster, but contrived to make the Sign of the Cross within its belly, thus splitting it in two. She is represented in art trampling on a dragon or quelling it by displaying a crucifix; her story, like George's, formed part of the immensely popular *Golden Legend*. Norwich is not the only place where she is associated with him and with dragon figures. For instance, at Bassingbourn (Cambridgeshire), an elaborately staged production of a play on 'The Holy Martyr St George' was performed on St Margaret's Day, 1511, and needless to say there was a dragon listed among the props. Similarly, at the church of St Margaret at Westminster, the churchwardens' account books several times allude to dragons, though without indicating whether it was in honour of their patroness or of St George that these were kept:

| 1491 | Item, received from the churchwardenes of | |
| | St Sepulchre's for the Dragon, | 2s. 8d. |
| | Item, paid for dressing of the Dragon and for | |
| | packthread, | −s. −d. |
| 1502 | Item, to Michell Wosebyche for makying | |
| | of viij Dragons, | 6s. 8d. |

The popularity of St George was so universal that plays and parades in his honour could be found far and wide, and were by no means limited to the churches of which he or St Margaret was patron.[6] For example, in 1519 at Wymondham in Norfolk, a Guild procession was held on the feast of St John the Baptist (24 June, Midsummer Eve), in which there appeared a statue of St George called 'the Riding George', together with the figure of a horse and that of a dragon. The making, repairing, or parading of dragons is also attested by brief references at various dates between 1467 and 1546 at Wigtoft (Lincolnshire), Heybridge (Essex), Walberswick (Suffolk), and at Leicester, where there was a Guild of St George. No details of the appearance or behaviour of these dragons survive.

There are disadvantages to St George's Day as a date for open-air festivities; the daylight hours are still far from their longest, and the weather can be chilly or uncertain. The summer months provided a series of more promising opportunities: May Day, Ascension Day, Whitsun, the Feast of Corpus Christi (i.e. the Thursday after Trinity Sunday), and the feast of St John the Baptist (24 June). In Catholic times, all these were observed as religious holidays, and in many places one or more of them was the occasion for merrymaking, including pageants, dances and plays, sometimes of great elaboration. One of the effects of the Reformation, as it gained strength and gradually began to change innumerable aspects of England's traditional life, was to force the abandonment of many old Catholic feast days, especially Corpus Christi and the feasts of saints not mentioned in Scripture itself. Another was to strive to break the link between worship and merrymaking, between the religious and the secular life of the community; hence the outrage felt by Stubbes at the sight of Morris men dancing in the church and churchyard.

## Civic Festivals

The effects of this change of attitude can be traced in the history of Snap of Norwich, who evolved from a religious dragon into a civic dragon. In Norwich, the St George's Guild was not dissolved, despite Edward VI's Act in 1547 abolishing guilds, fraternities and processions; instead, it changed its name slightly, and reconstituted its annual feast as 'the feast of the Mayor, Sheriff, Aldermen and Council', in the course of which the new Mayor was sworn into office. The candles and religious objects disappeared from the procession, and in 1558 it was laid down 'that there shall be neither George nor Margaret, but for pastime the Dragon to come and show himself as in other years'. At about the same period, the date was changed from St George's Day to the first Sunday after Trinity, then in 1572 to the Sunday before Midsummer Eve, then in 1584 to Midsummer Day; thereafter it remained a June festival, the high point of Norwich civic life, till well into the nineteenth century. Snap, who had begun his career as (officially at least) a mere attendant upon Saints George and Margaret, outlived them both in his new character as the Mayor's Dragon. Presumably his brothers in other towns made the same transition, for in 1694 Laurence Echard, in his commentaries on the plays of Plautus, talks of ' . . . Antick Figures with wide Mouths, like our Snap-Dragons for Mayors' Shows,' a remark which would be pointless if these were not a common sight.

Another town where the story of dragon-images can be followed over a long period of time is Chester, whose famous Midsummer Show is first recorded in 1498. This was a highly elaborate civic festival held on 23 June, in which a wide variety of fantastic figures took part, and which had also absorbed some of the religious tableaux and plays more usually associated with Corpus Christi. Among other items, there was a dragon. We first hear of it in the city records for 1564, when two painters were engaged to repair annually and have in readiness the processional figures, listed as four giants, a unicorn, a dromedary, a camel, a luce, an ass, a dragon, six hobby horses, and 16 naked boys. Presumably these last wore tight flesh-coloured costumes representing nakedness, and it was these costumes that needed repairs and attention from the painters.

Needless to say, the Puritans found all this most offensive, and did their utmost to suppress it:

> AD 1599, Henry Hardware, the Mayor, was a godly and zealous man; he caused the gyauntes in the midsommer show to be broken, and not to goe; the Devil in his feathers which rode for the Butchers he put away, and the cuppes and cannes, and the dragon, and the naked boys, but caused a man in complete armour to goe before the show in their stead.[7]

The innovation must have been unwelcome, for in 1601 a new Mayor 'set out the giants and Midsomer Show as it was wont to be kept', and in 1608 (when the Show was given a patriotic theme in honour of Prince Henry), there is a vivid description of the dragon:

> . . . very lively to behold, pursuing the savages, entering their denne, casting fire from his mouth; which afterwards was slaine, to the great pleasure of the spectators, bleeding, fainting and staggering, as though he endured a feelinge paine even at the last gaspe and farewell.

The 'savages' mentioned here are, I presume, the same as the 'naked boys' of 1564 and 1599, perhaps now envisaged as Red Indians or Wild Men. One must suppose, since no other personage is mentioned in connection with the dragon, that it is they who, after fleeing before him in the early stages of the pageant, eventually rally to attack him in the death scene so energetically described. They are thus true dragon-slayers, not merely attendants like the Whifflers and Fools who (as will be described) accompanied Snap of Norwich. Predictably, the Chester Midsummer Show was suppressed during the Cromwellian Commonwealth, but at the Restoration of Charles II the Mayor and Sheriffs decided to revive this 'ancient and laudable custom' and to pay the necessary expenses – 'all things are to be made new, by reason the old modells were all broken, as neere as may be lyke as they were before'. Among these renewals appears the item: 'For makynge new the dragon, and for six naked boys to beat at it, one pound sixteen shillings'. The expenses detailed on this occasion also reveal that whereas the hobby-horses needed only one boy apiece to carry and manoeuvre them, the larger animals, including the dragon, needed two grown men apiece; this shows that the Chester dragon must have been a bigger and more complicated creature than Snap.

Impressive though he was, the Chester dragon was only one figure among many in a large-scale pageant. No tale or tradition has been preserved to explain his presence, though a lifespan of one hundred and eighty years certainly indicates his popularity. For an explanatory legend centering upon one of these communal dragons, one can turn to the village of Burford in Oxfordshire, where, according to Camden's *Britannia* (1586), it was the custom of the inhabitants to make a dragon every year and carry it through the streets 'with great jollity' on Midsummer Eve, together with another figure representing a giant. This was alleged to commemorate a battle fought at Burford in A.D. 750 between Cuthbert or Cuthred of Wessex and Ethelbald of Mercia, in which the former was victorious and captured the latter's battle standard, which represented a golden dragon. This may be a true explanation, at any rate in the sense that it was locally believed to be true; on the other hand, it could be no more than a pseudo-explanation devised in post-Reformation times to justify the continuation of a medieval Catholic procession by imposing a new meaning upon it. If so, the Burford dragon would presumably have originally been associated with St George, as elsewhere, and the giant might have been meant as St Christopher, like the Giant of Salisbury. This, like so much else in this field, is mere speculation. However, the people of Burford were able to continue their jollifications well into the seventeenth century, since in 1705 Robert Plot in his *Natural History of Oxfordshire* speaks of the procession as having occurred within living memory. Sometimes it was held at Whitsun, sometimes at Midsummer, the patronal festival of Burford church being St John the Baptist's day.[8]

## Morris Men and Mummers

Meanwhile, what of the association between dragons and Morris dancers, which the indignant Stubbes had noticed as typical in village festivities in the 1580s? Our evidence concerning folk-dancing, mumming, hobby-horses, guisers, and all such aspects of working-class self-organised entertainments and rituals, is woefully patchy; the disapproval of the pious and the contemptuous silence of the educated are so much the norm throughout much of the seventeenth century and all the eighteenth that the occasional record or allusion is a mere flash illuminating one tiny corner among acres of dark ignorance. One such flash occurs in 1636, in a play by William Sampson entitled *The Vow Breaker, or the Fayre Maid of Clifton*, based on a real-life episode in Nottinghamshire.[9] In one scene, a group of characters is discussing arrangements to put on a Morris Dance, and they argue over who should play the hobby-horse – clearly this is a star part, involving imitation of a horse's movements, and also 'belts, plumes and braveries', and a horse head with its mane 'new shorne and frizzled'. At length Miles, the hobby-horse enthusiast, says to Ball, the organiser of the affair, 'Provide thou for the Dragon, and leave me for a Hobby-horse.' To which Ball replies, 'Feare not, I'll be a fiery Dragon,' and a third character adds, 'And I'll be a thundering St George.' The simultaneous presence of a dragon and a St George would almost certainly imply a combat between them, so it would seem that the entertainment being planned was not just a dance attended by grotesque animal figures, such as Stubbes described, but a mixture of dancing and dramatic action.

One widespread form of entertainment was the Mummers' Play, that curious comedy in rough-and-ready verse which has been traditionally performed in many parts of England, usually at Christmas or Easter. The basic plot of the 'Hero Combat' type concerns a series of single combats between a champion, usually called George, and various antagonists with fanciful names such as Bold Slasher, Turkish Knight, Black Prince, etc; one or more of the combatants gets killed, but is resuscitated by a comic Doctor. The hero, though generally entitled 'King' rather than 'Saint' George, is obviously the saint's secular descendant, who has inherited his popular reputation; in his opening speech he sometimes boasts of his most famous deed:

> I killed the fiery dragon and brought him to great slaughter
> And by this deed I won for me the King of Egypt's daughter.

Very occasionally, the Dragon himself appears as a character in the play and fights George; an example of this is a text from Burford (Oxfordshire),[10] where the Dragon at first overcomes George, who has to be revived by the Doctor, but then is killed by the hero in a second bout – and is not restored to life. Among the subsequent adversaries whom the Burford George defeats is a Giant, so it seems very likely that this village's version of the play has been influenced by the popularity of the processional dragon and giant which used to parade there at Midsummer. It must however be stressed that (contrary to what one would at first suppose) a dragon is among the rarest of the adversaries which the Mummers' Play provides for its George, and its presence is regarded by modern scholars as a sign of literary influence distorting folk tradition. There may have been practical reasons for the rarity of dragons in this context; to make an effective one involves a fairly elaborate head and body, preferably with a tail and wings too, and ideally also with some smoke or gunpowder effects. All this is manageable with the resources of a town or village pageant, but is far too expensive for a small group of farm labourers to arrange. However, one may also note some lines from an unusually elaborate Mummers' Play (suspected of literary influence and upper-class patronage) which was performed at Revesby Hall in Lincolnshire on 20 October 1779:

> We are come over the mire and moss,
> We dance an hobby-horse,
> A dragon you will see,
> And a wild worm for to flee.
> Still we are all brave jovial boys,
> And take delight in Christmas toys.[11]

Such brief glimpses and allusions do not amount to much; unless a great deal of relevant material has been lost (which is unfortunately quite possible), it seems as if the association between dragon-figures and Morris Men or Mummers had become rare by the eighteenth century.

### The Later Career of Snap

At Norwich, the career of Snap, the Mayor's Dragon, continued unbroken through the generations. But it was not literally the same Snap who led the Mayoral procession year after year, since wear and tear, not to mention gunpowder, meant that the effigy often needed repairs. Already in 1534 it had required 'canvas for his nekke and a new staffe', and from time to time a wholly new image had to be made. Thus in 1786 a publicity handbill announced that 'the old Snapdragon being dead, a young one is newly arrived here from Grand Cairo in Egypt, or somewhere else, which will make its first appearance, and the two Dick Fools will be dressed to attend His Monstrousness'. These Dick Fools were clowns dressed in painted canvas coats and red and yellow caps, adorned with cats' tails and small bells. There were also four or six Whifflers in Tudor costume, whirling their 'whiffles', i.e. swords, tossing them into the air, and skilfully catching them. The function of both the Whifflers and the Fools was to clear a way for Snap, controlling the crowd and preventing them from getting danger-ously close while Snap made his mock-aggressive rushes, clacking his jaws, swinging his tail, and opening his mouth to receive the coins tossed at him.

All good things come to an end. In 1835, Parliament passed a Municipal Reform Act which forbade all the pageants and processions which had so picturesquely enlivened the civic life of the older towns of England. 'The civic life of England, as such, is extinct' mourned a correspondent of *The Edinburgh Review* in 1843. In particular, he lamented the loss of the Norwich procession, where Snap was ' . . . as necessary to the Mayor as his gold chain . . . the delight and terror of the children . . . opening his wide and menacing jaws with no more felonious intent than the reception of a halfpence'. No longer could the Mayor and Mayor-Elect ride through the streets with their beadles, standard-bearers, mace-bearers, musicians, Councillors, Chaplain, and so forth, to attend a Cathedral service (during which Snap remained outside) and then invest the new Mayor in office, before proceeding to a banquet and ball. And Snap had no more official duties to perform.

But Snap did not disappear. The particular Snap holding office at the time was about forty years old, having been made around 1795, and he continued to appear on the streets of Norwich at irregular intervals until about 1850, when he retired into the Museum in Norwich Castle Keep, where he can be seen to this day. In honour of his past career, he is known as the Civic Snap. Meanwhile, various other Snaps had been constructed in and around Norwich, in close imitation of the original one. Two of them are described in Richard Lane's booklet *Snap the Norwich Dragon*, both being associated with mock guilds and mock mayors whose ceremonies were jocular imitations of the city's old solemnities. One was at a nearby village named Costessey[12] and the other in an area of Norwich itself called Pockthorpe. The latter held a June parade and a mock swearing-in, followed by sports and a fair, and had a mock guild which they had founded in 1772; the antics of their Snap were impressive, since the frivolous nature of the occasion gave him more opportunities for larking about than his official counterpart:

> Snap weaved his way among the crowd, or darted down the narrow lanes. With his menacing jaws, he grabbed the caps from people's heads and would only return them on payment of a penny or halfpenny . . . There are those among the senior citizens of Norwich who can remember the regular appearance of the Pockthorpe Snap during the early years of this century, right up until the First World War. Like generations of Norwich citizens before, they both feared him and loved him. His only evil intent was to steal the caps from the heads of boys and demand a penny ransom. The boys used to dare his snapping jaws by running under his mouth shouting: 'Snap, Snap, steal a boy's cap, give him a penny and he'll give it back.'[13]

The Pockthorpe Snap has now joined his Civic brother, whom he closely resembles, in the Castle Keep Museum; there too is yet a third Snap, recently discovered in a dilapidated condition in a Norwich pub, and possibly also originating in the Pockthorpe area. And still the tradition continues, with a Norwich Snap Festival in 1976, for which schoolchildren made and paraded their own miniature dragonets.

### Dragons and Hobby-horses

Thus we have evidence, patchy but consistent, by which to trace the activities of 'hobby-dragons' from the fifteenth century to the present day; we see them featured in religious plays and processions, and in civic pageants (especially at Midsummer); sometimes they are associated with Morris Men or, more rarely, with Mummers. There are thus some striking similarities between these dragons and the more numerous and better documented hobby-horses of England and Wales, whose history, distribution and functions have recently been authoritatively analysed in E. C. Cawte's *Ritual Animal Disguise*. Both types of creature entertained by mock aggressiveness and unruly behaviour; both could be used for collecting money or gifts in kind, often by 'swallowing' coins in their jaws; both enjoyed a peak of fashionable popularity in the fifteenth and sixteenth centuries; both could readily become a focus of local pride; even in construction there are resemblances between Snap and the 'tourney' hobby-horses (i.e. those that are built up on a framework slung round a man's waist), while workable and noisy jaws are a common feature of many types of hobby-beasts. At the same time, there are equally important differences which must not be overlooked. The hobby-horse (or sheep, or bull, or stag) belongs to a widespread and ancient group of midwinter visitants found in many parts of Europe, whose alarming antics almost certainly were originally rituals to ensure the renewal of fertility. Hobby-dragons, on the other hand, often appeared in a Christian context, and so far there is only one piece of evidence hinting at the existence of some ritual or sport involving dragon images that is earlier than the fifteenth century (see pages 117–18). Also, whereas the hobby-horses were firmly entrenched in rural areas, where small groups of working men spontaneously kept the tradition alive, the dragons flourished best under the patronage of a church, a guild or a civic authority. It is probably fair to say that hobby-dragons were usually deliberately devised for officially approved public entertainments (rather than inherited from deep-rooted folk traditions), and that those who designed and manipulated them were imitating the appearance and behaviour of the already well-known hobby-horses.

However, the reverse influence might also sometimes have occurred, and it may not be irrelevant to consider two famous hobby-horses, still extant, which show some features unusual in the breed. These two are the Padstow Old Oss and the Minehead Sailors' Horse (in Cornwall and Somerset respectively). They are untypical among British hobby-horses in that they appear on May Day, are geographically isolated, and are constructed as strikingly individual variations on the 'tourney' type – whereas other British hobby-animals appear in winter or at Easter, occur in well-defined regional clusters, and are almost all constructed on the 'mast' principle. Both these horses parade through the streets of their towns, accompanied by musicians, collecting money from the onlookers; both are grotesque figures, having no realistic resemblance to a horse; both are adept at 'skirmishing among the crowd', and in former times were more markedly aggressive in their pranks than they are today. The Padstow Oss, whose body is a black cloth hanging from a six-foot circular frame balanced on the operator's shoulders, chases girls and tries to catch them under the cloth, which in the old days was smeared with blacking. The Minehead Horse is eight foot long, also worn on the shoulders; it has a long tail of rope and ribbons with which its attendants used to entrap people, and until about 1880 it also had a head with snapping jaws, to bite those who would not pay. The Minehead Horse used to be accompanied by masked men called Gullivers, who would thwack people with a boot if they refused to give the horse money; the Padstow Oss is accompanied by dancers, in particular by one nowadays called the Teaser, who guides its movements. The Padstow Oss is famous for the clear fertility symbolism of its ritual, especially for the way in which it periodically sinks down to die and then leaps back into life in a most impressive manner; nevertheless both he and the Minehead Horse also give pleasure by their mock-aggressive behaviour – a common feature shared by hobby-horses and dragons.

But the real reason for including these two horses here is the faint whiff of dragon that can be discerned in some of the incidental stories told about them, or in details of the performance surrounding them. A local anecdote recently collected at Minehead alleges that once upon a time the port was threatened by Viking raiders, but that some sailors disguised a boat to look like a sea-serpent, and so frightened them off; the Sailors' Horse is supposed to represent not a horse at all, but this boat in its reptilian disguise.[14] (The actual appearance of the 'Horse' does not look in the least like a sea-serpent, but neither does it look much like a horse!) At Padstow, St George has somehow got himself mixed up in the traditions about the Oss; one nineteenth-century collector reports local stories about how he visited Padstow on horseback, and how an unfailing spring gushed out where his horse pawed the ground. Even more curiously, a nonsense verse which is sung as a dirge whenever the Oss 'dies' begins:

> O where is St George? O where is he-o?
> He's out in his long-boat all on the salt sea-o.

To these fragmentary items one can add the more substantial historical fact that Minehead and Padstow are both connected with dragon-quelling saints whose legends have already been given (pages 55–6): Padstow takes its name from St Petroc, while Minehead is only four miles from Carhampton, where St Carantoc founded his monastery. Moreover, it is obligatory for the Minehead Horse to visit Dunster Castle in the course of its rounds, and this castle is traditionally identified with the stronghold to which St Carantoc led the captive dragon. Another of its stopping places is actually called Dragon's Cross. Again, until the 1930s the Padstow Oss used to 'drink' from a certain pool and splash water over the onlookers; water-splashing is common in luck-bringing or fertility-inducing rituals, but one is also reminded of how St Petroc thoroughly sprinkled his sick dragon with holy water (page 56). The legends about these saints would have been extremely familiar in the localities concerned during the Middle Ages. I am therefore tempted to speculate: did Minehead and Padstow once have religious pageants showing their patron saints leading a captive dragon in triumph, as so many towns in Catholic Europe did? Have their present hobby-horses inherited features from these former Catholic pageants? One such feature could well be the springtime date of their performance, rather than the winter one favoured by most hobby-horses; St Carantoc's feast-day is 16 May, and St Petroc's is 4 June, so if celebrations formerly held on these days were being secularised (or unofficially continued, in defiance of a prohibition) they might well have ended up on the nearby public holiday of May Day. In the absence of church records or other documents to show how Minehead and Padstow celebrated their patronal festivals in medieval times, these questions must remain without definitive answers; the notion that the horses of these two towns are (at least partially) descended from older dragons is a tempting theory, but one which falls short of proof.

It would in any case be quite wrong to say that hobby-horses in general derive from hobby-dragons; on the contrary, dragons were never as widespread, let alone as ancient, as horses, bulls, and stags as disguises in seasonal customs. In this connection, it is significant that in all the many legends of dragons and their slayers that have been so far surveyed in this book, there is not the least trace of a seasonal element; the dragon is never said to have committed its depredations at a particular time of year, nor to have been killed on a particular day. But since there is no rule without an exception, a tradition very recently collected in Essex must be mentioned here: A dragon is said to come up out of the River Stour, between Wormingford and Dedham, in May-time every year, to take a young maiden.[16] There is no killing in this tale, which asserts that the dragon is still alive and active. Apart from this one modern instance, however, the legends show no seasonal aspects; and as for the association of hobby-dragons with the Midsummer season at Norwich, Chester, Burford and elsewhere, this seems to mean nothing more significant than that Midsummer was the date chosen by these towns for their annual merrymaking.

Thus, whatever may be true of hobby-horses, the hobby-dragon cannot be interpreted as a seasonal figure whose 'slaying' or 'dying' is a magic ritual ensuring renewed fertility. The resemblance between the two types of monsters depends on other factors – their boisterous, unrestrained and aggressive behaviour, their comic aspects, and the focus they provide for local patriotism. Both embody the carnival spirit, in which destructive or bawdy instincts are allowed a temporary and well-limited outlet; both are just sufficiently alarming in their grotesque appearance to inspire a comfortable self-congratulation in those who feel no fear of them – for instance, in the boys daring Snap to snatch their caps off. It would be most interesting to know whether the hobby-dragons were regarded as luck-bringers, as hobby-horses are, but unfortunately the scanty sources never mention this aspect. Foreign parallels, however, make it likely that they were. For instance, the famous French she-dragon, La Tarasque of Tarascon (a most fearsome-looking figure, first mentioned in 1465, still extant, and requiring several men and a boy to manoeuvre) was very definitely regarded as a luck-bringer; as recently as 1948, people thought it lucky to touch it during the parade, and even better if one could pull one of its spikes off. Similarly, at Mons in Belgium there is a processional dragon escorted by 'wild men', which attacks the onlookers with its long tail, whereupon they respond by trying to pluck a hair from it for luck. Louis Dumont, in his penetrating study *La Tarasque* (1951), sums up the reasons for the figure's popularity under two main aspects: it is a symbol and focus of the town's sense of its identity and unity; and its mock-aggressive assaults on the crowds offer a healthy release to destructive instincts, transforming them into a vigorous, beneficent and luck-bringing energy. Everything that we know of the English hobby-dragon, 'skirmishing among the crowd', 'the delight and terror of the children' and of adults who 'both feared him and loved him', shows that what is true of La Tarasque must also have been true of him.

## A Medieval 'Dragon game'?

The evidence considered so far all tends to date the rise of the hobby-dragon to the late Middle Ages, the earliest fixed date being the foundation of the Guild of St George in Norwich in 1389, and the majority of the allusions to dragon figures coming in the fifteenth and sixteenth centuries. But can this really be the beginning of the story, considering that dragons had always had a place in Christian symbolism, and before that in pre-Christian myths and legends? Are there any traces of non-ecclesiastical ceremonies or sports involving dragons in early Medieval England, before the period of St George's great popularity, of the lavish Mystery Plays, and of the big civic spectacles like that of Chester?

There is one piece of evidence bearing upon this problem, namely a carved capital dating from about 1130 which came from the Abbey Church at Reading, now in Reading Museum; it has been closely studied and interpreted by Mrs Ellen Ettlinger, whose analysis I follow here.[17] Each of the four faces of the capital shows two human figures and two dragons locked in combat, but the human beings are not the same ones each time; facial details reveal that they are eight different persons, two being adult men, three youths, and three young boys. The two dragons, however, seem to be the same ones all the time, though their poses differ in each scene; a line at the junction of their heads and necks is taken to indicate that they are not intended as live beasts but as models, with moveable wings and legs, open jaws, and protruding tongues. However, there is nothing in the carving to show where the operator controlling them was placed. The method of combat is a very unexpected one; in each scene, the human beings are tugging at the tongues of their respective dragons, dragging them farther and farther out of the jaws, until not only the tongues and windpipes but eventually also the lungs and hearts have been ripped bodily out and held in triumph. None of the men, youths and boys carry weapons; where their legs can be seen, it seems they are wearing peculiar thick trousers ending in hoof-like attachments. Mrs Ettlinger argues that what is here shown is a form of dramatic entertainment in which a team of men, youths, and boys, wearing strange garments that give them a partially animal appearance, attack and 'kill' artificial dragon-figures with their bare hands. Since 'eleventh- and twelfth-century sculptors usually depicted well-known themes for the instruction or for the entertainment of church-goers', she deduces that 'the subject represented on the capital is a cheerful and popular one'; a parallel from an episode in the medieval Icelandic *Saga of Hrolf Kraki* suggests that it was a form of sport designed to demonstrate courage, self-reliance and resourcefulness, and that it was derived from initiation tests imposed on young warriors in earlier periods.

If this interpretation of the Reading capital is accepted, it becomes of great value for the glimpse it affords of an early and quite non-religious type of medieval entertainment involving dragons. It anticipates the spectacular scenes in the Chester pageant, where the team of 'naked boys' was pursued by the monster-effigy, until at length they fought and destroyed it. Also, there are interesting points of similarity with three features which we have already encountered in several of the local legends discussed in earlier chapters: the anonymous, non-aristocratic, non-chivalrous heroes; their odd and rather grotesque garments; their even odder and more grotesque method of slaying, which nevertheless has its basis in brutal realism, since it is a known method of slaughtering small animals, e.g. piglets. True, neither these garments nor this form of killing can be matched among the surviving legends, but they clearly belong to the same world of mingled humour, excitement, and earthy practicality as that with which the tales have made us familiar. At the same time, the idea of a test of manly valour recalls those tales in which the hero is raised in status as reward for his deed. Thus the Reading capital points to the fairly early existence of a dramatised custom, or a well-known story (or, of course, both), whose features anticipate aspects of the later local legends, but whose roots lie in the more archaic world of warriors' initiation rites. It is much to be hoped that further close examination of the corpus of medieval carving may reveal additional examples of such subjects.

# CHAPTER SEVEN

# Problems, Theories and Conclusions

The majority of people, on hearing a traditional tale about some imposs-ible event such as a dragon-slaying, at once become curious to know how it can have originated. 'Sheer imagination' is often rejected as an unsatisfy-ing answer, since it is felt that the value of the story is far greater if one can show that, despite appearances, 'there was something in it after all'. If the tale concerns their own locality, this reaction is all the stronger. When Louis Dumont was gathering material about La Tarasque in 1948, he found that almost all the informants he questioned in Tarascon had adopted some theory about what the dragon of their town's custom and legend had 'really' been. The theories were of two kinds; first the naturalistic ones, claiming that La Tarasque had been some real but unfamiliar beast (e.g. a crocodile or a turtle) which later stories had exaggerated; the others sought an explanation in symbolism, some favour-ing mythological interpretations and others Christian or political/ historical ones. Essentially, all such theories are formed by concentrating upon some particular phase of the long, complex history of dragons outlined in Chapter I, and seeing in this the sole and sufficient explanation of the local legend under discussion.

## Far-Flung Parallels

The quest for origins is, however, fraught with many difficulties, chief among them being that the local legend whose origin one is seeking almost always has far more parallels elsewhere than its hearers are aware of, so that it would be rash to propose an explanation for it without taking these parallels into account. Thus, one should not construct a theory about British dragon tales which could not also cover their many European parallels. Continental dragon-lore can match all the main themes we have been considering: the knight as hero, the saint as hero, the peasant or criminal as hero; the noble combat, the ingenious trick combat, the combat with tragic ending; the hero's reward; the strong local associations; the material objects constituting 'evidence'. As regards processional and festal dragons, the Continent can still produce several to match our surviving Snap, and many more are known to have existed until the seventeenth and eighteenth centuries.

It is not too difficult to account for these similarities on the assumption that British and Continental dragon-lore was all derived from a common source or sources during the Middle Ages, circulating through an area which at that time had many cultural traits in common. What is more astonishing is to find similar themes turning up in widely separated times and places – not merely broad general themes such as 'hero slays devastating monster', which are well-nigh universal, but sharply individualised motifs such as the spiked armour or container which the monster attacks, the hero destroying the monster from within, or the strange foods that choke the monster to death. Here, at random, are a few of these far-flung parallels: in Greek myth, Herakles jumps down a sea-monster's throat and hacks his way out from within; in the Indian epic, *Ramayana*, monkeys do the same, swelling themselves up inside sea-dragons and splitting them; in an American Indian legend, Coyote lets himself be swallowed by the water-monster Nashlah while carrying wood and pitch, with which he sets Nashlah's heart on fire;[1] in the Persian epic, *Shah Nameh*, Isfadiar has a closed chariot studded with spearheads and knives in which he sits while the dragon swallows it with the usual fatal result, and is spewed to safety in its death-throes;[2] in the apocryphal part of the *Book of Daniel*, Daniel makes a dragon burst by tossing balls of pitch, fat and hair into its mouth. None of these stories except the last would have been known in Medieval Britain and Europe; they are cited here simply to show how ancient and widespread is the notion of the trick combat, and consequently how complex any theory about its origin and diffusion would have to be.

It is also instructive to observe how easily the same motif can be adapted to varying levels of seriousness, according to the context in which it appears; few things, it would seem, are intrinsically serious or intrinsically comic. Thus the common motif 'hero swallowed by monster' is found in religious myth, in heroic epic, in fairy tales, in saints' lives, in tall tales such as the popular American cycle about Paul Bunyan, and in the humorous fantasy of Kipling's story 'How the Whale Got his Throat'. The yawn or sneeze which forces the monster to open his jaws and so enables the hero to attack its vulnerable inner parts is featured in the earliest and most serious of cosmic dragon-myths, those of Indra and of Marduk. It re-appears in 1932 as the one authentic-sounding detail in a heavily romanticised version of the Sussex legend of the Knucker of Lyminster, in which, as a desperate last resort, the wounded and fallen hero tickles the dragon's nose with a blade of wild oats to make him sneeze, and then stabs into his open jaws.[3] It is reasonably certain that local men who told the story thus were telling it for laughs, though the authoress who put it into magazine form surrounded it with so much high-toned language that the final effect sits very uneasily between two stools. As so often, one would need to hear the actual narration of a folktale to assess its effect, and without it one is helpless; for instance, is the baldness of Herakles on emerging from the monster's belly (page 27) a deeply serious symbol of his being reborn, as some have maintained? Or a symbol of the horror he has undergone, as when we say, to round off some tale of a man who had seen a ghost, that 'his hair had gone white in the night'? Or was it funny to the Greeks, as it now is to us? Where such problems abound, the question of how seriously people believed in dragons can be almost as insoluble as the question of how dragons originated, and each tale must be individually assessed in the light of its cultural context.

Bearing these warnings in mind, we may turn to some more manageable questions. How old are the surviving British dragon legends? How far do they support the various theories about dragon origins put forward by scholars or by people in general? What social or psychological functions do they fulfil? Why have they survived?

## Dating the Legends

In judging the age of a legend or custom, it is almost always permissible to assume that the earliest recorded mention of it was preceded by an indefinite period of unrecorded existence. Sometimes, indeed, the only reason one hears about something is because someone is complaining about it or trying to suppress it; for example, in the early years of the eleventh century, Abbot Ealdred of St Albans, in the course of gathering stones for rebuilding his Abbey, 'flattened as far as he was able' what had apparently long been a famous local cavern and ravine named Wormenhert in which a dragon was reputed to have lived, 'so dispelling for ever the traces of the serpent's lair'.[4] Much pre-Conquest tradition must have been lost after 1066, dying away unrecorded because of the indifference of Norman chroniclers; much Catholic tradition was actively suppressed at the Reformation and during subsequent generations of Puritan influence. In assessing the dates of surviving dragon-legends and known dragon-customs, one notices that in several cases the first allusions to them come in the fifteenth and sixteenth centuries (see Appendix C): I think it likely that the major formative period in the development of British dragon-lore as we now know it began in the later Middle Ages, more archaic tales and customs having left only a few enigmatic traces such as place names (e.g. Knucker Hole, Drakelow), and the carved scene on the Reading capital.

Various lines of argument lend support to this dating. One is the link with heraldry,[5] for the important group of legends linking dragon-slayings with family crests could not have arisen until after – maybe several generations after – the adoption of the crest concerned; hereditary crests began to come into use in the thirteenth century. Dragons had been used earlier as decorations on baronial seals (beginning *c*.1180), at which stage they were drawn as two-legged; the four-legged dragon first appears in English heraldry around 1400. A second major factor was the cult of St George, at its peak of popularity at the end of the fourteenth century and in the fifteenth; the connections of dragons with religious pageants and dramas and the parallels between them and the hobby-horses also point to a period at the close of the Middle Ages as the likely starting-point for their rise to popularity.

The part played by church carvings and tombs offers only a rather uncertain guide to dating. There are some cases, but not many, where the carving seems to allude to an existing story or custom, which therefore obviously must pre-date its representation; the most important of these is the dragon-fight on the twelfth-century capital from Reading, while another is the rood-screen at Norton Fitzwarren, from about 1500 (page 57). But far more often the legend has simply misinterpreted a carving which originally was of religious significance, or was a heraldic emblem, or a pure grotesque, or is so worn as to be mysterious; in all such cases, one can say no more than that the tale arose later, possibly much later, than the date of the object to which it is attached.

It would of course be ludicrous to argue that no dragon legends whatever existed in Britain in the first half of the Middle Ages (indeed, the evidence of place-names and of saints' lives would soon demolish such a theory), but it seems that the main formative period for tales of types we have been considering began in the later Middle Ages and probably continued through the Tudor and Elizabethan periods, with successful story-patterns spreading from place to place by imitation. It is possible (as was suggested in Chapter 5) that a growing ignorance about older Catholic art and traditions during the seventeenth and eighteenth centuries favoured the growth of another crop of stories designed to explain monuments which had become puzzling. However, since the tales first recorded at these later dates follow the same patterns as the older ones, this secondary period of legend-building must be considered as essentially imitative. Appendix C gives a list of dates for legends recorded before the nineteenth century; it must however always be remembered that in a field so badly documented as this, a particular legend may have existed for generations before anyone thought to mention it in print, so that a story which looks comparatively late could be in fact just as old as one which had the luck to be recorded earlier.

It is also of course quite possible for a complex legend to develop by stages over a long period of time. This must have happened in the case of the Lambton Worm, where the dragon-slaying itself can be presumed to be Medieval or Tudor, but the idea of the curse to the ninth generation can only have evolved after its 'fulfilment', i.e. after several Lambtons had died elsewhere than in their beds. Henderson mentions two killed in battle during the Civil War, and another who died in his carriage in 1761; it was he who was alleged to be the ninth and last victim of the curse. So the curse-motif, and with it the motif of the promise to the witch and the attempted trickery with the dog, must have been added to the main dragon-slaying plot after 1761. Probably the motif of fishing on a Sunday is also a later addition or alteration, since it follows Protestant, not Catholic, teaching about what is allowed on Sundays; the Catholic equivalent (if there was one in the early stages of the tale) would have been that Sir John missed Mass, not that he went fishing, for pleasure was not in itself forbidden to Catholics on Sundays. Most probably, however, the idea of Sir John's guilt had no place in the oldest version, for no other dragon-slayer is considered to be in any way to blame for the existence of the monster he slays. Thus this legend, more complex than the rest in its structure and thought, has reached its present form by the accretion of episodes over several centuries; interestingly, the popular song based on it has restored (or preserved?) a simpler story line (pages 141–2).

## General Theories of Origin

*The Mythological Theory* – The next point to be considered is the relation between the individual local tales and the various general theories proposed about dragons, in order to see how far (if at all) the tales support the theories, or the theories cast helpful light on the tales. It must be remembered that it is not scholars alone who seek explanations and weave theories; people living in the neighbourhood of a dragon-legend are eager to speculate upon it, and to pass on their ideas as to what it all really meant.

Among scholars, one favourite theory has been some form of mythological symbolism. During the nineteenth century, when nature myths attracted the most interest, the dragon was variously interpreted as a symbol of darkness, drought, floods, eclipses or storms; nowadays, the stress is on myths about cosmic creation, so the link between the dragon and primeval chaos is stressed. This theory is based upon, and directly relevant to, the early mythical material described in Chapter 1; some scholars have also tried to apply it to the interpretation of specific local legends of more recent date. For example, French folklorists have more than once pointed out that many of the legends in France about saints subduing dragons are set in valleys that were marshy or subject to flooding, and have proposed that 'slaying the dragon' in these cases meant draining the marshes or bridging the river, the Church having encouraged these practical good works. This theory does not seem very convincing, at any rate not in the English context. I would find it hard to believe that whoever first devised the tale of Sir John Lambton and the Worm was 'really' saying that the Wear is a dangerous river and that the Lambtons built a bridge across it – nor, as far as I know, has such a suggestion ever been made. The chief usefulness of the mythological theory when applied to local legends is that it offers an explanation for the very frequent association of local dragons with a watery habitat, as mentioned in Chapter 2. However, this point, though a striking one for scholars, seems to have little importance in the minds of those who actually told the stories. Probably, indeed, they would not even have noticed it, since normally each storyteller would know only the tale of his own district, and so would have had no reason to draw general conclusions about watery habitats. In any case, mythical symbolism about chaos and the destructive forces of nature is remote from British material in its medieval and post-medieval forms.

*Naturalistic Theories* – Naturalistic theories have a far wider appeal. The suggestion is very frequently made, both by writers and by people hearing or telling a dragon legend, that not only the general concept of such monsters but also the particular local example being discussed originated from the misunderstanding of some natural object or phenomenon. Possibilities proposed include crocodiles, tropical snakes or lizards escaped from menageries or brought home dead from abroad; stranded whales; fossils; and the ever-popular hypothesis of the surviving dinosaurs. Apart from this last, which on scientific grounds seems untenable, the others must be admitted to be indeed possibilities, in the sense that one must concede that such a misunderstanding could theoretically have occurred. On the other hand, there are over seventy localised British stories about dragons, and it seems rather strained to suggest that every one of them arose from somebody's hasty and panic-stricken glimpse of a strayed crocodile or dead whale, or even that half or a quarter of them did. So the real question is not so much whether it might have happened as whether there is any positive indication within the story itself to show that it did.

I know of only two instances where the hypothesis of an escaped tropical snake or lizard looks plausible or helpful. The first is a vague account of a 'serpent' brought to England by Barbary merchants which escaped and haunted the region of Hornden, Essex, till it was killed by Sir James Tyrell, who was wearing a mirror on the breast of his armour. The second is an apparently sober and objective description in a pamphlet published in August 1614 of a creature allegedly then to be seen in St Leonard's Forest, Sussex:

> This serpent (or dragon, as some call it) is reputed to be nine feete, or rather more, in length, and shaped almost in the form of an axletree of a cart: a quantitie of thickness in the middest, and somewhat smaller at both endes. The former part, which he shootes forth as a necke, is supposed to be an elle long; with a white ring, as it were, of scales about it. The scales along his backe seem to be blackish, and so much as is discovered under his bellie, appeareth to be red . . . it is also discovered to have large feete, but the eye may be there deceived . . . There are likewise upon either side of him discovered two great bunches so big as a large foot-ball, and (so some thinke) will in time grow to wings . . . He will cast his venom about four rodde from him . . . His food is thought to be, for the most part, in a conie-warren, which he much frequents . . .  [6]

Confronted with such circumstantial details, claimed to be from the eyewitness accounts of 'John Steele, Christopher Holder, and a Widow Woman dwelling near Faygate', the reader has only two explanations to choose from: either there was really something there (a gorged python or a large tropical lizard have been proposed); or the publisher was indulging in a journalistic hoax, exploiting public credulity, love of sensation, and the difficulty of checking up on alleged marvels in remote country districts. If the latter is true, he may have found inspiration in the older legend of St Leonard and the Dragon (page 48). This pamphlet, though received at the time with some mockery, has now passed into accepted Sussex lore; it is frequently quoted in books about the county, and has recently been chosen as one of a series of Sussex folktales for illustration on a set of matchboxes. Perhaps, in this one case, there was once some unfortunate reptile which escaped from a menagerie and which, before it froze to death, passed into local legend, but on balance a publisher's hoax seems the more likely, as also in the case of the Flying Serpent at Henham (page 41).

Another type of naturalistic explanation turns on the fact that unusually dramatic displays of aurora borealis, meteors, and strange forms of lightning were once interpreted by the ignorant as apparitions of flying fiery dragons. A well-known early instance is the entry for the year 793 in the *Anglo-Saxon Chronicle*, which links dragons and aurora borealis, seeing both as ominous:

> This year came dreadful forewarnings over the land of the Northumbrians, terrifying the people most woefully. These were immense sheets of light rushing through the air, and whirlwinds, and

fiery dragons flying across the firmament. These tremendous tokens were soon followed by a great famine, and not long after, on the sixth day before the ides of January in the same year, the harrowing inroads of heathen men made lamentable havoc in the Church of God on Holy Island, by rapine and slaughter.

Strange lights in the sky were still being called 'fiery drakes' in Scotland 1000 years later; in an area near Aberdeen in 1793, a contemporary records:

In the end of November and beginning of December last, many of the country people observed very uncommon phenomena in the air (which they call dragons) of a red fiery colour, appearing in the north, and flying rapidly towards the east; from which they concluded, and their conjectures were right, that a course of loud winds and boisterous weather would follow.[7]

Granted that people believed these meteorological phenomena to be dragons, are they likely to have affected individual local legends? Only, I think, in the sense that they bolstered up a general belief in the existence of dragons; a strange light in the sky is too remote, unearthly, and ominous to be easily transmuted into the kind of dragon found in local tales – one that had once lurked just round the corner, so to speak, and had been effectively slaughtered by the local hero. The difference in emotional impact is, on a smaller scale, rather like the difference between the supernaturally terrifying Devil of religious legends and the homely, comic Devil who tosses rocks or digs dykes across the landscape in so many folktales.

Before leaving naturalistic explanations and turning to symbolic ones, mention should perhaps be made of certain new types of pseudo-scientific and occult theories which can be found in many present-day popular works.[8] These are written by and for people who already, on other grounds, believe in the reality of phenomena outside the scope of orthodox science, such as flying saucers, currents of electrical earth-force, and evil psychic entities localised in certain spots; they then interpret the dragons of folklore as examples of the phenomena or forces concerned. Thus, to take some typical examples of this way of thinking, the dragons of Bures and of Newcastle Emlyn (pages 67, 84) have been claimed as flying saucers because of the mention of their impenetrable hides, and the dragon flying across the Exe Valley (page 35) has been interpreted as a line of earth-force linking two hills. Such interpretations offer a fascinating insight into the psychological urges which drive men towards belief in the remote, the mysterious, the semi-secret, the barely-possible, the esoteric and exciting;

those for whom our landscape is the scene for earth-forces, ley lines, and UFO sightings, are in their own way bestowing glamour and importance upon it, just as the devisers of the dragon legends did.

*Theories of Moral Symbolism* – If British dragons are too modern to be seen in terms of mythological thought, and if they show no signs of being inspired by encounters with actual animals, are they to be explained in terms of Christian symbolism and moral teachings? Certainly there was a very strong stimulus to be found in the lives of saints and in church art and pageantry, where dragons so frequently appear as symbols of the Devil, of heathenism, and of moral wickedness; certainly, too, the fact that they are mentioned in the Bible would have seemed a guarantee that they really could exist. It is beyond doubt that if the Church had not made so much use of dragons in its art and literature, they would never have flourished in fairytales and local legends to the extent that they have. Three tales, those of St Carantoc, St Petroc and St Columba, occur in Church writings relating to the period of conversion in Britain, and it is quite likely that in these the defeated monsters were deliberately intended to symbolise the evil heathenism put to flight by the saint. This, however, is not the same thing as saying that the populations of the regions converted by these saints were in the habit of worshipping snakes – such a theory would require far stronger evidence than the routine equivalence of Dragon/ Demon which is so common in hagiography, and whose roots lie in the Bible and in the writings of the Fathers of the Church, not in any attempts accurately to represent the practices of pre-Christian religions. For the Church, dragon-slaying was simply a broad general symbol of the triumph of holiness over temptation, of good over evil; indeed, this is still a very living concept in our own time, as a glance at children's literature soon makes plain.

And yet, after surveying the mass of British dragons, it does not seem accurate to say that the predominant impression they make is that they are symbols for religious and moral evil. True, they are dangerous, destructive beasts; they kill cattle and human beings, they are often venomous, and they inspire great fear. But what is equally marked is the total absence of religious or moral notions from almost all these tales; for instance, it is never said that the dragon had been supernaturally sent to punish the sins of a community (although in one version of the Strathmartin story the girls eaten are Sabbath-breakers), nor that it is itself a demon, nor that the victims had been praying for a deliverer to come, nor even (except in the case of saints and also at Castle Carlton and Lambton Castle) that the hero himself prayed for strength or divine help before going into battle. This predominantly secular tone is not an inevitable feature of local folktales;

there are certain types of story which do make moral or religious points, for instance those about towns that have sunk into lakes because of their wickedness, girls turned to stone for dancing, or treasures lost through swearing. So dragon legends with ethical overtones would have been quite a possibility, if the traditional storytellers had wished to evolve a sub-type of this sort; the almost complete absence of such components is therefore a legitimate objection to the view that sees dragons chiefly as carrying a religious significance.

Here, however, we must consider the two stories where a religious element is markedly present, although the hero is not a saint, namely those of Piers Shonks and Sir John Lambton. In the case of Piers, it will be recalled, the Devil was so enraged at his slaying of the dragon that he swore he would catch Piers' soul, 'whether he was buried inside the church or outside it', but Piers avoided the danger by having his tomb in the thickness of the wall. Here, then, is a traditional story in which the Devil and the dragon are represented as allies, the one seeking to avenge the other. Its force is much weakened, however, by the fact that the anecdote about wall-tombs often occurs on its own elsewhere, without any connection with dragon-slaying; at Brent Pelham the tomb had features which attracted to it both a dragon legend and a cheat-the-Devil legend, and a simple link of cause-and-effect was devised to cover the join (see page 93). Despite its ingenious Latin verse about the two serpents, the tradition at Brent Pelham is only rather superficially religious.

In the tale of Sir John Lambton and his Worm, the religious element is far more thoroughly integrated into the fabric of the story, at any rate in the line of tradition represented by Henderson's account and by the anonymous Victorian pamphlet reprinted in Appendix A. 'The young heir of Lambton led a dissolute and evil course of life,' we are told in the latter, 'equally regardless of the obligations of his high estate and the sacred duties of religion. According to his profane custom he was fishing on a Sunday . . . ' He was cursing, too, and on catching the immature Worm he exclaimed, 'I think I've catched the Devil himself!' Here, and here only in the corpus of British tales, we find a hint that dragon and Devil are to be identified, for it was a widespread belief that the Devil would appear to those who broke the Sabbath in various ways, including fishing, and also to those who swore. Later in the pamphlet we hear that 'the young heir of Lambton had repented him of his former sins' and gone to fight the infidel; the 'Sybil' whom he consults tells him 'that he himself had been the cause of all the misery which had been brought upon the country', and his promise to kill the first thing he would meet after victory is presented as 'a solemn vow in the chapel of his forefathers'. Also, 'the afflicted household were devoutly engaged in prayer during the combat'.

After all this high moral tone, it is a great contrast to turn to the popular song on the same subject, which probably dates from the later nineteenth century (Appendix A, page 141); this wholly omits the witch, the promise and the curse, and treats the fishing scene with casual flippancy:

> One Sunday Morning Lambton went
> A-fishing in the Wear,
> And catched a fish upon his hook
> He thought looked verry queer.
> But whatten a kind of fish it was
> Young Lambton couldn't tell;
> He wouldn't fash to carry it home,
> So he hoyed it in a well.

It has already been pointed out that the Lambton legend must be a composite, additional elements having been dovetailed onto its basic plot at a later period. It is probably to these later developments that the pamphlet version (and Henderson's similar one) owes the earnest preoccupation with sin and expiation, and the idea of presenting the dragon's arrival as the result of the hero's moral lapses. These attitudes reflect Protestant piety; they have only one small and feeble parallel in the corpus of British dragon legends (i.e. the Sabbath-breaking girls in one version of the tale from Strathmartin), and they cannot be taken as an essential insight into the meaning of dragon legends.

*Theories of Historical Symbolism* – The fourth type of interpretation is the historical/political one. According to this school of thought, where one finds a localised story of a dragon-fight, one should see in it a memory, imaginatively expressed, of some long-ago battle in which the defeated enemy is now symbolised by a slain monster. Local historians have been, and still often are, inclined to view their legends in this light: they are likely to point out that Celtic chieftains were sometimes called 'Pendragon', or that Saxon kings used dragon banners, or that Viking ships had dragon figureheads, and to argue that therefore the legend recalls the defeat of whichever of these enemies is the most appropriate to the area. Sometimes it is not just historians but the local population which adopts this interpretation, as at Burford in the sixteenth century (page 109). Political allegory expressed in terms of animals certainly has plenty of medieval precedents; one famous example in our field is the tale of how Merlin as a boy foretold the wars of Britons against Saxons in terms of a battle between a red dragon and white one. Some of our local stories do look as if they might have been meant to commemorate some local skirmish, possibly simply one against men from a nearby village. One candidate for this role would be the curious affair at Bures mentioned in a medieval chronicle (page 67), and another odd story from the same region:

> A most unusual battle is alleged to have taken place near Little Cornard on the afternoon of Friday, September 26, 1449, according to a contemporary chronicle now in Canterbury Cathedral. In a marshy field on the Suffolk/Essex border, two fire-breathing dragons engaged in a fierce, hour-long struggle. The Suffolk dragon was black and lived on Kedington Hill, while the dragon from Essex was 'reddish and spotted', and came from Ballingdon Hill, south of the River Stour. Eventually the red dragon won, and both creatures returned to their own hills, 'to the admiration of many beholding them'. The site of the battle is known locally as Sharpfight Meadow.[9]

Battle theories have been tentatively put forward by some writers to explain the stories at Mordiford, Lyminster and Norton Fitzwarren. In none of these cases, however, is there any evidence other than the legend itself to show that a battle did take place in the area, so the argument becomes circular; moreover, except in one case (the Uffington White Horse) there is no correlation between the sites of dragon legends and the sites of known battles of, for instance, the Viking invasions or the various medieval revolts and civil wars. The theory of battle allegories does, however, have two things to recommend it. One is that it could explain why the sites of dragon tales tend to be in river valleys or coastal districts, since these are places of strategic importance. The second is that it undeniably corresponds well to popular psychology, for the dragon-as-enemy is a notion which springs to mind as readily as the dragon-as-evil, and can indeed blend easily with it. There is a neat modern example of this double symbolism in the church at Wormingford; it is a window given as a thank-offering for the safe return of soldiers from the Second World War, and the subject chosen for it is the men of Bures triumphantly putting a dragon to flight.[10]

One story, 'The Dragon of Wantley' (first printed in 1685) has a claim to be thought historical in a different sense. In the fourth edition of his *Reliques of English Poetry* (1794), Bishop Percy added to this poem an explanatory note from a local informant to the effect that it was composed as a satire about a lawsuit over tithes early in the reign of James I.[11] According to this, the dragon was Sir Francis Wortley, holder of the disputed tithes, and More was an attorney who set up a lawsuit against him on behalf of some of the neighbouring gentry; the spiky armour was said to be a document 'full of names and seals' in which these men all pledged themselves to oppose Sir Francis. It is an amusing notion, which fits in well with the tone of rumbustious parody in these verses. Yet, seeing how many parallels the poem has with traditional tales elsewhere, it is obvious that whoever wrote it had a sound knowledge of dragon legends and did not invent his plot out of the blue; more likely, there already was a legend either at Wantley or nearby, which a clever writer versified with additional touches which alluded satirically to the lawsuit.

Thus the various general theories about the origins of dragons turn out to be only occasionally helpful in interpreting particular local stories, as soon as we look at the latter individually. One can indeed often observe some concrete object whose presence was, in one sense, the origin of the legend, as has been shown in the examples given in Chapter 5; but if one seeks for a deeper interpretation of the significance (as opposed to the occasioning stimulus) of the legend, none of the proposed theories of origins seems satisfying for more than a handful of cases. Perhaps the search for the 'original meaning' is a dead end, however tempting it looks; it would be better to turn from a past which is inaccessible, and to ask instead what function the legend is fulfilling in the form in which it now exists, and what social and psychological factors we can discern as favouring its survival.

## Social Functions: Family Pride and Local Identity

Here it is helpful to consider how these tales can be fitted into wider categories of story-types, instead of viewing them as we have done up to now as an isolated group characterised solely by the fact that they are all about dragons. First, many of them fit into a type whose pattern consists of the killing or subduing of a dangerous wild beast of any species, real or imaginary, generally resulting in honour and reward for the hero. In England the beast is most often a boar, but it could also be a wolf, lion, griffin, cockatrice, or even a wild cow; effigies, local place-names, and family coats of arms may all play a part, just as in the dragon tales. A good example is the story of how Roger de Ferry slew the Brawn of Brancepeth (County Durham), which was said to be the last boar in Britain, by trapping it in a branch-covered pit, and stabbing it to death;[12] the family descended from him had a boar as their crest, and a tomb reputed to be his in Kirk Mannington churchyard is said to show a sword and a spade. The story from Bishop Auckland which has been told above (page 62) in its dragon version is also commonly told in a boar version, showing how the animals involved can be accepted as interchangeable equivalents. Something similar could be said in the case of saints' legends; alongside the special sense in which overcoming a dragon means overcoming the Devil, there is also a wider pattern in which a saint demonstrates the power of holiness by expelling, subduing, taming, or giving orders to, a wild beast of any dangerous sort (St Francis of Assisi and the wolf, St Jerome and the lion, St Patrick and the snakes). Viewed against this background, the dragon no longer appears endowed with a unique significance, but becomes one out of many dangerous beasts on whom a secular hero can prove his courage, or a saintly one his faith.

One particular group of dragon-slaying legends can be slotted into another broad category, that of the legend whose function is to explain a coat of arms or crest by some particularly dramatic tale, designed to emphasise the courage or strength of the founding ancestor. There are many such; two examples will suffice. To explain the red hand on the arms of the O'Neills, it is said that their ancestor was taking part in a race by boat across a lake, for which the prize was the High Kingship of Ireland, and which would be won by the man whose hand first touched the opposite shore; to be sure of winning, he cut off his own left hand and hurled it onto the shore. To explain the muzzled bear of the Breretons, it is said that their ancestor, under sentence of death, was offered a chance of life if he could make a muzzle strong enough to control a wild bear, and put it on the beast himself, which he was able to do. Legends of this type have a strong, clear-cut function, to enhance the family prestige; they also have the best possible chances of survival, being learnt not only by each new generation of the family but by very many who came into contact with them, and being constantly reinforced by the visual presence of the heraldic device they set out to explain.

Thirdly, almost all the dragon legends offer explanations of material objects, place-names, or topographical features, as has been shown in Chapter 5. They thus form part of the extremely numerous class of local legends which simultaneously foster and satisfy a community's curiosity about its past, and about its environment. The subject matter of such tales is immensely varied, including both elements drawn from the naturalistic world (treasures, lost villages, traditions about battles, famous robbers, etc), and supernatural elements (fairies, giants, the Devil, etc). But whether their material is realistic or fantastic, it is always dramatic, exciting, and often amusing, too. They seem to function on two levels. On the more superficial, they offer a memorable and entertaining 'explanation' of some place or object that seems mysterious; more subtly, they foster the community's awareness of and pride in its own identity, its conviction that it is in some respect unusual, or even unique. That the lord of the manor should be descended from a dragon-slayer, that a dragon should once have roamed these very fields, or, best of all, that an ordinary lad from this very village should have outwitted and killed such a monster – these are claims to fame which any neighbouring community would be bound to envy. And even when no one believes the story any longer, it still can function as a kind of mascot, laughed at yet loved, giving its name to pubs and carefully passed on in local guidebooks. Everyone would like the story to be as old as possible, as unique as possible, and with some basis in fact, if at all possible; hence the many 'real explanation' theories about dragons, and hence, too, the disappointment some people clearly feel on finding out that theirs is not the only dragon tale.

It is no surprise, communal rivalry being what it is, to observe neighbouring villages each trying to snatch a share of the glory – Wormingford, for instance, annexing a tale which in the oldest source is merely stated to come from 'near Bures', or a Lyminster narrator hotly asserting that his hero Jim Puttock came from the small hamlet Wick, just next to Lyminster, rather than from the market town of Arundel a couple of miles away, as some ill-informed people were claiming. And, imitation being the sincerest form of flattery, it is pretty certain that dramatically effective tales were deliberately copied from one place to another, with small changes of detail to adapt them to their new setting, just as the prestige of the Civic Snap at Norwich led to the making of other dragon-effigies in and near that town.

It is interesting how often it is the dragon, rather than the hero, upon whom this sense of community pride is focused. This is obvious at Norwich, where the citizens kept their Snap going even when Sts George and Margaret were discarded, and it is equally clear in many of the tales. 'I'll tell you about the Worm,' not 'I'll tell you about Sir John,' is the promise of the folk-singers round Lambton Castle; the Lyminster Knucker and the Mordiford Dragon keep their identities whatever disagreement there may be about who slew them, and how; at Ludham and at Henham, figures of the local dragon were sold at the annual fair. All this must appear illogical if one views dragons either as symbols of destructive evil or allegories of beaten enemies, and yet it is undeniable that an attitude of affectionate amusement and appreciation crops up again and again in the tales which seem the closest to oral tradition, as opposed to heavily literary treatments like Marlowe's version of the Castle Carlton story or the Victorian pamphlet on the Lambton Worm. Of course, one must not forget that, despite this sympathy, the dragons always end up dead, and we are meant to cheer.

## Psychological and Aesthetic Pleasures of Dragon Tales

How is one to assess these paradoxes? What exactly were the pleasures to be got from telling and hearing tales of dragon slayings? With what mixture of feelings did people think of dragons? Perhaps the underlying attitudes were akin to those of big-game hunters, who relish describing every detail of the strength, cunning and dangerousness of their quarry, and display a mixture of respect, hearty familiarity, and affection in talking of it, until it is hard to decide which pleases them most – the merits of the beast, or their own merit in destroying it. Then again, dragon legends must have been a harmless outlet for aggressive instincts, allowing the hearers first to enjoy the picturesquely exaggerated destructiveness of the monster, and then to identify with the hero who so bravely or cleverly destroys it and re-establishes the safe normality of everyday life. And again, there must have been pleasure in half believing for a moment that a truly weird and wonderful creature once enlivened with its presence a humdrum corner of the countryside. All these are conscious or semi-conscious sources of enjoyment; I must leave to others, better versed in Freudian or Jungian psychology than I, the question of what subconscious needs a dragon legend might fulfil.[13]

Nor must it be forgotten that oral storytelling is an art, and gives aesthetic satisfaction to performer and audience alike. In the case of these tales, their aesthetic qualities consist partly in a sense of drama and partly in a sense of humour (often, indeed, in both). For, although 'The Dragon of Wantley' stands alone as an example of slap-stick farce, there are plenty of other tales where an understated humour is a dominant note, and it goes without saying that any dragon-slaying is an exciting affair, whether it be achieved in heroic combat or by ingenious trickery. It is interesting to observe how contrasting treatments of a basic plot exist side by side in the same place; one variant may be jocular and the other moralising; one may have an upper-class and the other a working-class hero; one may have a triumphant and the other a tragic outcome. But each in its own terms is an exciting, aesthetically satisfying tale.

The humour of the 'trick' slayings depends to some extent on the contrast with the heroic ones, which were apparently regarded as the norm, even though they are, in fact, rather less frequent, and almost always less detailed. If the listeners are expecting St George or a knight in shining armour, as their knowledge of religious legends and tales of chivalry would predispose them to do, then the farm lad with the pudding or the shepherd with his crook or the criminal in his spiked barrel will be all the more enjoyable by contrast. There is also much relish for ingenuity for its own sake, in the astonishing and complicated devices many heroes resort to, and especially in the laughable contrast between the redoubtable dragons and the humble domestic objects such as peats, puddings and parkins which are their undoing. Here there may well be an element of poetic justice to add one's satisfaction – a poisonous dragon poisoned, a fire-breathing one choked by smoke from smouldering peat, a greedy one incapacitated by the stone or pudding or parkin he so rashly gulped down. Or again, the hero himself may be turned into a ludicrous-looking monster, a sort of parody-dragon, as he encases himself in a barrel or a glass case, plasters himself with pitch or with birdlime and ground glass, flourishes a smoking stinking peat, or dons his spiky armour. The point is quite explicit in 'The Dragon of Wantley', where More scares everyone by looking like 'some strange outlandish hedgehog'. Anyone whose sense of humour includes a liking for the bizarre, and who does not mind a mild touch of schoolboyish bloodthirstiness mingled with it, will find these traditional tales well fitted to his tastes.

At the same time, the trick tales have their more serious side as well, for they teach the value of courage just as effectively as the heroic combats do, together with the need for a cool head and ready wits. A German scholar recently commented, in the course of an analysis of the story of Sigurd/ Siegfried and the dragon Fafnir, on the method Sigurd used, which was to hide in a pit over which the monster would be bound to crawl on its way to the river to drink, and to stab it from below.[14] This, he tells us, was an ancient trick used by hunters when going after large or dangerous prey; far from being an easy way out, it required the utmost coolness, patience and bravery – so much so that it might well be used as an initiation test for young warriors. Many centuries separate our dragon tales from the world of early Germanic warriors, and themes which were once treated in deep earnest are now generally told with a twinkle in the eye. Yet even in the most light-hearted modern folktale, a dragon-slayer still needs to be brave and resourceful, and maybe a little unfair in his methods, just as Sigurd was.

> And now, lads, I'll hold my gob,
> That's all I know about the story
> Of brave Sir John and what he done
> Wi' the awful Lambton Worm.

# The Wonderful Legend of the Lambton Worm

The young heir of Lambton led a dissolute and evil course of life, equally regardless of the obligations of his high estate, and the sacred duties of religion. According to his profane custom, he was fishing on a Sunday, and threw his line into the river to catch fish, at a time when all good men should have been engaged in solemn observance of the day. After having toiled in vain for some time, he vented his disappointment at his ill success in curses 'loud and deep' to the great scandal of all who heard him on their way to Holy Mass, and to the manifest peril of his own soul.

At length he felt something extraordinary 'tugging' at his line, and in the hope of catching a large fish, he drew it up with the utmost skill and care, yet it required all his strength to bring the expected fish to land. But what was his surprise and mortification when, instead of a fish, he found that he had only caught a worm of most unseemly and disgusting appearance, and he hastily tore it from his hook and threw it into a well hard by (still known by the name of Worm Well).

He again threw in his line, and continued to fish; when a stranger of venerable appearance, passing by, asked him, 'What sport?' To which he replied, 'I think I've catched the Devil,' and directed him to look in the well. The stranger saw the worm, and remarked that he had never seen 'the like of it' before – that it was like an eft, but that it had nine holes on either side of its mouth, and 'tokened no good'.

The worm remained neglected in the well, but soon grew so large that it became necessary to seek another abode. It usually lay in the daytime coiled round a rock in the middle of the river, and at night frequented a neighbouring hill, twining itself around the base, and it continued to increase in length until it could 'lap' itself three times round the hill (i.e. the Worm Hill near Fatfield).

It now became the terror of the neighbourhood, devouring lambs, sucking the cows' milk, and committing every species of injury on the cattle of the affrighted peasantry. The immediate neighbourhood was soon laid waste, and the worm, finding no further support on the north side of the river, crossed the stream towards Lambton Hall, where the old Lord was then living in grief and sorrow; the young heir of Lambton having repented him of his former sins, and 'gone to the wars in a far distant land', according to some 'to wage war against the infidels'.

The terrified household assembled in council, and it was proposed by the steward, a man 'far advanced in years, and of great experience', that the large trough which stood in the courtyard should be filled with milk. The monster approached, and eagerly drinking the milk, returned without inflicting further injury, to repose around its favourite hill.

The worm returned next morning, crossing the stream at the same hour, and directing its way to the hall. The quantity of milk to be provided was soon found to be that of 'nine kye'; and if any portion of this quantity was neglected or forgotten, the worm showed the most violent signs of rage, by 'lashing' its tail round the trees in the park, and tearing them up by the roots.

Many a gallant knight of undoubted fame and prowess had sought to slay this monster, 'which was the terror of the whole countryside'; and it is related that in these mortal combats, though the worm was frequently cut asunder, yet the several parts had immediately reunited, and the valiant assailant never escaped without the loss of life or limb, so that, after many fruitless and fatal attempts to destroy the worm, it remained, at length, in tranquil possession of its favourite hill – all men fearing to encounter so deadly an enemy.

At length, after seven long years, the gallant heir of Lambton returned from the wars of Christendom, and found the broad lands of his ancestors laid waste and desolate. He heard the wailings of the people, for their hearts were filled with terror and alarm. He hastened to the hall of his ancestors, and received the embraces of his aged father, worn out with sorrow and grief, both for the absence of his son, whom he had considered dead, and for the dreadful waste inflicted on his fair domain by the devastations of the worm.

He took no rest until he crossed the river to examine the worm, as it lay coiled around the base of the hill; and being a knight of tried valour and sound discretion, and hearing the fate of all those who had fallen in the deadly strife, he consulted a Sybil on the best means to be pursued to slay the monster.

He was told that he himself had been the cause of all the misery which had been brought upon the country, which increased his grief, and strengthened his resolution; that he must have his best suit of mail studded with spear blades, and take his stand on the rock in the middle of the river, commend himself to Providence and to the might of his sword, first making a solemn vow, if successful, to slay the first living thing he met; or, if he failed to do so, the Lords of Lambton for nine generations would never die in their beds.

He made the solemn vow in the chapel of his forefathers, and had his coat studded with the blades of the sharpest spears. He took his stand on the rock in the middle of river, and unsheathing his trusty sword, which had never failed him in his hour of need, he commended himself to the will of Providence.

At the accustomed hour the worm uncoiled its lengthened folds, and leaving the hill, took its usual course towards Lambton Hall, and approached the rock where it sometimes reposed. The knight, nothing dismayed thereat, struck the monster on the head with all his might and main, but without producing any visible effect, than by irritating and vexing the worm, which, closing with the knight, clasped its frightful coils around him, and endeavoured to strangle him in its poisonous embrace. But the knight was provided against that unexpected extremity, for the more closely he was pressed by the worm, the more deadly were the wounds inflicted by his coat of spear blades, until the river ran with a crimson gore of blood. The strength of the worm diminished as its efforts increased to destroy the knight, who, seizing a favourable opportunity, made such good use of his sword that he cut the monster in two; the severed part was immediately carried away by the force of the current; and the worm being thus unable to reunite itself, was, after a long and desperate conflict, finally destroyed by the gallantry and courage of the Knight of Lambton.

The afflicted household were devoutly engaged in prayer during the combat; but on the fortunate issue, the knight according to promise, blew a blast on his bugle to assure his father of his safety, and that he might let loose his favourite hound, which was destined to be the sacrifice. The aged parent, forgetting everything but his parental feelings, rushed forward to embrace his son.

When the knight beheld his father he was overwhelmed with grief. He could not raise his arm against his parent, yet hoping that his vow might be accomplished, and the curse averted, by destroying the next living thing that he met, he blew another blast on his bugle. His favourite hound broke loose, and bounded to receive his caresses, when the gallant knight, with grief and reluctance, once more drew his sword, still reeking with the gore of the monster, and plunged it into the heart of his faithful companion. But in vain. The prediction was fulfilled, and the Sybil's curse pressed heavily on the house of Lambton for nine generations.

Popular tradition has handed down to us, through successive generations, with very little variation the most romantic details of the ravages committed by these all-devouring worms, and of the valour and chivalry displayed by their destroyers. Without attempting to account for the origin of such tales, or pretending to vouch for the matters of fact contained in them, it cannot be disguised that many of the inhabitants of the County of Durham in particular still implicitly believe in these ancient superstitions. The Worm of Lambton is a family legend, the authenticity of which they will not allow to be questioned. Various adventures and supernatural incidents have been transmitted from father to son, illustrating the devastation occasioned, and the miseries inflicted, by the monster – and marking the self-devotion of the Knight of the Lambton family, through whose intrepidity the worm was eventually destroyed. But the lapse of centuries has so completely enveloped in obscurity the particular details, that it is impossible to give a narration which could in any degree be considered as complete.

The present history has been gleaned with much labour on the banks of the Wear, on both sides, near the scene of action, from both sexes, and the result faithfully recorded . . . It is not now possible to account satisfactorily for the origin of the Lambton Worm legend. The story has been repeated without variation for centuries, and we must be content to leave it in its wonted obscurity.

Anonymous pamphlet, published by T. Arthur and A. Everatt, Newcastle-on-Tyne, *c.*1875. Facsimile reprint, Frank Graham, Newcastle-on-Tyne, 1968

## The Lambton Worm

One Sunday morning Lambton went
　　A-fishing in the Wear,
And catched a fish upon his hook
　　He thought looked verry queer,
But whatten a kind of fish it was
　　Young Lambton couldn't tell;
He wouldn't fash to carry it home,
　　So he hoyed it in a well.

*Chorus*
　　Whisht, lads, and hold your gobs,
　　And I'll tell you all an awful story;
　　Whisht, lads, and hold your gobs,
　　And I'll tell you 'bout the Worm.

Now Lambton felt inclined to gan
　　And fight in foreign wars,
He joined a troop of Knights that cared
　　For neither wounds nor scars,
And off he went to Palestine,
　　Where strange things him befell,
And he very soon forget about
　　The queer worm in the well.

*Chorus*
　　Whisht, lads, . . .

Now t'Worm got fat and growed and growed,
　　And growed an awful size;
He'd great big teeth, a great big gob,
　　And great big goggly eyes;
And when at nights he crawled about
　　To pick up bits of news,
If he felt dry upon the road,
　　He milked a dozen cows.

*Chorus*
　　Whisht, lads, . . .

This fearful Worm would often feed
    On calves and lambs and sheep,
And swallow little bairns alive
    When they lay down to sleep,
And when he'd eaten all he could
    And he had had his fill,
He crawled away and lapped his tail
    Ten times round Lambton Hill.

*Chorus*
    Whisht, lads, . . .

The news of this most awful Worm
    And his queer goings-on
Soon crossed the seas and reached the ears
    Of brave and bold Sir John.
So home he came and catched the beast
    And cut him in two halves,
And that soon stopped him eating bairns
    And sheep and lambs and calves.

*Chorus*
Whisht, lads, . . .

So now you know how all the folks
    On both sides of the Wear
Lost lots of sheep and lots of sleep
    And lived in mortal fear;
So let's have one to bold Sir John
    That saved the bairns from harm,
Saved cows and calves by making halves
    Of the famous Lambton Worm.

*Chorus*
    Now, lads, I'll hold my gob,
    That's all I know about the story
    Of bold Sir John and what he done
    Wi' the awful Lambton Worm.

> Folksong, anonymous and of unknown date;
> probably nineteenth century

## *The Knucker of Lyminster*

The hedger laid his gloves atop of the carefully wiped bill, and settling himself on the bank where the crisp tongues of the primroses had begun to push aside the rustle of drifted leaves, began to untie his 'elevenses'.

'They do say,' he observed deliberately, as he spread his red and white spotted handkerchief across his knees, 'that a dunnamany years ago there was a gert dragon lived in that big pond there – Knucker his name was, and Knucker Hole we calls it today. And thisyer ole dragon, you know, he uster go spannelling about the Brooks by night to see what he could pick up for supper, like – few horses, or cows maybe – he'd snap 'em up soon as look at 'em. Then bymby he took to sitting top o' Causeway, and anybody come along there, he'd lick 'em up, like a toad licking flies off a stone.

So what with that, and him swimming in the river otherwhile and sticking his ugly face up again the winders in Shipyard when people was sitting having their tea, things was in a tidy old Humphrey up Ar'ndel way, no bounds.

So the Major of Ar'ndel, as was then, he offered a reward for anyone as 'ud put an end to 'en. I misremember how much 'twas, but something pretty big, I reckon. Howsomever, everybody was so feared on 'en, that they was onaccountable backward in coming forward, as you might say.

So Mayor, he doubled the reward; and this time a young chap from Wick put up for it. Now some people says he was an Ar'ndel man, but that ain't true. Young Jim Puttock his name was, and he came from Wick. I've lived at Toddington all my life, so I reckon I oughter know. Sides, my great-aunt Judith, what lived down along there where you turns up by they gert ellum trees, just tother side o' the line, uster say that when she was a gal there was a man lived 'long o' them as was courting a gal that 'ventually married a kind of descendant of this Jim Puttock.

Let be how 'twull, this Jim Puttock he goos to Mayor and tells him his plan. And Mayor he says everybody must give en what he asks, and never mind the expense, 'cause they oughter be thankful anyway for getting rid of the Knucker.

So he goos to the smith and horders a gert iron pot – 'bout *so* big. And he goos to the miller and asks en for so much flour. And he goos to the woodmen and tells 'em to build a gert stack-fire in the middle of the Square. And when 'twas done he set to and made the biggest pudden that was ever seen. And when 'twas done – not that 'twas quite done – bit sad in the middle, I reckon, but that was all the better, like – they heaved 'en onto a timber-tug, and somebody lent him a team to draw it, and off he goos, bold as a lion.

All the people followed en as far as the bridge; but they dursen't goo no furder, for there was old Knucker, lying just below Bill Dawes's place. Least, his head was, but his neck and body-parts lay all along up the hill, past the station, and he was a-tearing up the trees in Batworth Park with his tail.

And he sees thisyer tug a-coming, and he sings out, affable-like, 'How do, Man?'

'How do, Dragon?' says Jim.

'What you got there?' says Dragon, sniffing.

'Pudden,' says Jim.

'Pudden?' says Dragon. 'What be that?'

'Just you try,' says Jim.

And he didn't want no more telling – pudden, horses, tug, they was gone in a blink. Jim 'ud 'a gone too, only he hung on to one o' they trees what blew down last year.

''Tweren't bad,' says Knucker, licking his lips.

'Like another?' says Jim.

'Shouldn't mind,' says he.

'Right,' says Jim, 'bring 'ee one 'sartenoon.' But he knew better'n that, surelye.

Afore long they hears en rolling about, and roaring and bellering fit to bust hisself. And as he rolls, he chucks up gert clods, big as houses, and trees and stones and all manner, he did lash about so with his tail. But that Jim Puttock, he weren't afeard, not he. He took a gallon or so with his dinner, and goos off to have a look at en.

When he sees en coming, old Knucker roars out: 'Don't you dare bring me no more o' that there pudden, young man!'

'Why?' says Jim. 'What's matter?'

'Collywobbles,' says Dragon. 'It do set so heavy on me I can't stand up, nowhows in the wurreld.'

'Shouldn't bolt it so,' says Jim. 'But never mind, I got a pill here, soon cure that.'

'Where?' says Knucker.

'Here,' says Jim. And he ups with an axe he'd held behind his back, and cuts off his head.'

The hedger took a long pull at his tea-bottle, and lapsed into silence.

'That's all?' said I.

'That's all, sir. But if you goos through that liddle gate there into the churchyard, you'll see his grave. By the porch, left-hand side, in the corner like, between the porch and the wall of the church.'

And sure enough, the grave is there, and covered with a great coped slab of Horsham stone. But it is without inscription, and though many are proud to show it, this hedger was the only one I ever met who gave the hero 'a local habitation and a name'. To all the rest, he was simply 'the man who killed the Dragon'.

Charles G. Joiner, 'The Knucker of Lyminster',
*Sussex County Magazine* III, 1929, 845–6

[Note: The gravestone has since been moved inside the church, and stands against the wall of a side chapel.]

## The Dragon of Wantley

Old stories tell, how Hercules
　　A dragon slew at Lerna,
With seven heads, and fourteen eyes,
　　To see and well discern-a:
But he had a club, this dragon to drub,
　　Or he had ne'er done it, I warrant ye;
But More of More Hall, with nothing at all,
　　He slew the dragon of Wantley.

This dragon had two furious wings,
　　Each one upon each shoulder;
With a sting in his tail, as long as a flail,
　　Which made him bolder and bolder.
He had long claws, and in his jaws
　　Four and forty teeth of iron;
With a hide as tough as any buff,
　　Which did him round environ.

Have you not heard how the Trojan horse
　　Held seventy men in his belly?
This dragon was not quite so big,
　　But very near, I tell ye.
Devoured he poor children three,
　　That could not with him grapple;
And at one sup he ate them up,
　　As one would eat an apple.

All sorts of cattle this dragon did eat,
　　Some say he ate up trees,
And that the forest sure he would
　　Devour up by degrees;
For houses and churches were to him geese and turkies;
　　He ate all, and left none behind,
But some stones, dear Jack, which he could not crack,
　　Which on the hills you will find.

In Yorkshire, near fair Rotherham,
  The place I know it well;
Some two or three miles, or thereabouts,
  I vow I cannot tell;
But there is a hedge, just on the hill's edge,
  And Matthew's house hard by it;
There and then was this dragon's den,
  You could not chuse but spy it.

Some say, this dragon was a witch;
  Some say, he was a devil,
For from his nose a smoke arose,
  And with it burning snivel,
Which he cast off, when he did cough,
  In a well that he did stand by;
Which made it look just like a brook
  Running with burning brandy.

Hard by a furious knight there dwelt,
  Of whom all towns did ring,
For he could wrestle, play at quarter-staff, kick,
                         cuff and huff,
  Call son of a whore, do anything more;
By the tail and the mane, with his hands twain,
  He swung a horse till he was dead;
And that which is stranger, he for very anger
  Ate him all up but his head.

These children, as I told, being eat,
  Men, women, girls and boys,
Sighing and sobbing, came to his lodging,
  And made a hideous noise:
'O save us all, More of More Hall,
  Thou peerless knight of these woods;
Do but slay this dragon, who won't leave us a rag on,
  We'll give thee all our goods.'

'Tut, tut,' quoth he, 'no goods I want;
  But I want, I want, in sooth,
A fair maid of sixteen, that's brisk and keen,
  With smiles about the mouth;

Hair black as sloe, skin white as snow,
　With blushes her cheeks adorning;
To anoint me o'er night, e'er I go to fight,
　And to dress me in the morning.'


This being done, he did engage
　To hew the dragon down;
But first he went, new armour to
　Bespeak at Sheffield town;
With spikes all about, not within but without,
　Of steel so sharp and strong;
Both behind and before, arms, legs, and all o'er,
　Some five or six inches long.


Had you but seen him in this dress,
　How fierce he looked and how big,
You would have thought him for to be
　Some Egyptian porcupig.
He frighted all, cats, dogs and all,
　Each cow, each horse and each hog;
For fear they did flee, for they took him to be
　Some strange, outlandish hedgehog.


To see this fight, all people then
　Got up on trees and houses,
On churches some, and chimneys too,
　But these put on their trousers,
Not to spoil their hose. As soon as he rose,
　To make him strong and mighty,
He drank by the tale six pots of ale,
　And a quart of aqua-vitae.


It is not strength that always wins,
　For wit doth strength excell;
Which made our cunning champion
　Creep down into a well,
Where he did think this dragon would drink,
　And so he did in truth;
And as he stooped low, he rose up and cried 'Boh!'
　And hit him in the mouth.

'Oh,' quoth the dragon, 'pox take thee, come out,
    Thou disturbst me in my drink.'
And then he turned, and shat at him -
    Good lack! How he did stink!
'Beshrew thy soul, thy body's foul,
    Thy dung smells not like balsam;
Thou son of a whore, thou stinkest so sore,
    Sure thy diet is unwholsome'

Our politic knight, on the other side,
    Crept out upon the brink,
And gave the dragon such a douse
    He knew not what to think.
'By cock,' quoth he, 'say you so, do you see?'
    And then at him he let fly
With hand and foot, and so they went to't,
    And the word was 'Hey, boys, hey!'

'Your words,' quoth the dragon, 'I don't understand.'
    Then to it they fell at all
Like two boars so fierce, if I may
    Compare great things with small.
Two days and a night, with this dragon did fight
    Our champion on this ground;
Though their strength it was great, their skill it was neat,
    They never had one wound.

At length the hard earth began to quake,
    The dragon gave him a knock,
Which made him to reel, and straightaway he thought
    To lift him as high as a rock,
And thence let him fall. But More of More Hall
    Like a valiant son of Mars,
As he came like a lout, so he turned him about,
    And hit him a kick on the arse.

'Oh,' quoth the dragon, with a deep sigh,
    And turned six times together,
Sobbing and tearing, cursing and swearing,
    Out of his throat of leather;

'More of More Hall! Oh thou rascal!
    Would I had seen thee never!
With the thing at thy foot, thou hast prick'd my arse-gut,
    And I'm quite undone for ever.


'Murder, murder!' the dragon cried,
    'Alack, alack for grief!
Had you but missed that place, you could
    Have done me no mischief.'
Then his head he shaked, trembled and quaked,
    And down he laid and cried;
First on one knee, then on back tumbled he,
    So groaned, kicked, shat, and died.


First recorded in an anonymous broadside,
*A True Relation of the Dreadful Combat between
More of More Hall and the Dragon of Wantley*, 1685.

# Assipattle and the Muckle Mester Stoor Worm

Assipattle was the youngest of seven sons. He lived with his father and mother and brothers on a fine farm beside a burn. They all worked hard except Assipattle, who could be persuaded to do little. He lay beside the big open fire in the farm kitchen, caring nothing that he became covered with ashes. His father and mother shook their heads over him; his brothers cursed him for a fool and kicked him. Everyone hooted with mirth when Assipattle told, of an evening, stories of incredible battles in which he was the hero.

One day awful news reached the farm. It was said that the muckle mester Stoor Worm was coming close to land. The Stoor Worm was the most dreaded creature in all the world. People grew pale and crossed themselves when they heard his name, for he was the worst of 'the nine fearful curses that plague mankind'. If the earth shook, and the sea swept over the fields, it was the Stoor Worm yawning. He was so long that there was no place for his body until he coiled it around the earth. His breath was so venomous that when he was angry and blew out a great blast of it, every living thing within reach was destroyed and all the crops were withered. With his forked tongue he would sweep hills and villages into the sea, or seize and crush a house or ship so that he could devour the people inside.

When he came close to the country where Assipattle lived, and began to yawn, people knew that he must be fed, otherwise he would get into a rage and destroy the whole land. The news was that the king had consulted a wise man, a spaeman, about what must be done. After thinking a while, the spaeman said that the only way to keep the Stoor Worm happy was to feed him on young virgins, seven of them each week. The people were horrified by this, but the danger was so appalling that they consented.

Every Saturday morning seven terrified girls were bound hand and foot and laid on a rock beside the shore. Then the monster raised his head from the sea and seized them in the fork of his tongue and they were seen no more.

As they listened to what the king's messenger, who had brought the news, had to tell, the faces of Assipattle's father and brothers grew grey and they trembled, but Assipattle declared he was ready to fight the monster. All through the years, he bragged, he had been saving his strength for just this. His brothers were furious and pelted him with stones, but his father said sadly, 'It's likely you'll fight the Stoor Worm when I make spoons from the horns of the moon.'

There were even more dreadful things for the messenger to relate. He said that the people of the country were so horrified by the deaths of the loveliest and most innocent girls that they demanded some other remedy. Once again the king consulted the spaeman, who declared at long last, with terror in his eyes, that the only way to persuade the monster to depart for good was to offer him the most beautiful girl in the land, the Princess Gem-de-Lovely, the king's only child. Gem-de-lovely was the king's heir, and he loved her more than anyone else. But the people were so frantic with grief at the loss of their own children that the king said, with tears rolling down his cheeks, 'It is surely a wonderful thing that the last of the oldest race in the land, who is descended from the great god Odin, should die for her folk.'

There was only one possible way of saving the princess, so the king asked for sufficient time to send messengers to every part of his realm. They were to announce that the princess would become the wife of any man who was strong enough and brave enough to fight the monster and overcome him. The wedding gift to the champion would be the kingdom itself and the famous sword Snikkersnapper that the king had inherited from Odin.

Thirty champions had come to the palace (said the messenger who had halted his weary horse at Assipattle's farm), but only twelve of them remained after they had seen the Stoor Worm. Even they were sick with fear. It was certain the king had no faith in them. Old and feeble as he was, he had taken the sword Snikkersnapper out of the chest behind the high table and had sworn he would fight the monster himself rather than let his daughter be destroyed. His boat was pulled down from its noust and was anchored near the shore, so as to be ready when he needed it.

Assipattle listened eagerly to all this, but no one heeded him. The messenger mounted his horse and slowly rode away. Soon the father and mother went to bed. From where he lay beside the flickering fire, Assipattle heard them saying that they would go next day to see the fight between the king and the monster. They would ride Teetgong, who was the swiftest horse in the land.

How was it that Teetgong could be made to gallop faster than any other horse? asked the mother. It was a long time before Assipattle's father would tell her, but at last, worn out by her questions, he said, 'When I want Teetgong to stand I give him a clap on the left shoulder; when I want him to run quickly I give him two claps on the right shoulder; and when I want him to gallop as fast as he can go I blow through the thrapple [windpipe] of a goose that I always keep in my pocket. He has only to hear that and he goes like the wind.'

After a while there was silence and Assipattle knew they were asleep.

Very quietly he pulled the goose thrapple out of his father's pocket. He found his way to the stable, where he tried to bridle Teetgong. At first the horse kicked and reared, but when Assipattle patted him on his left shoulder he was as still as a mouse. When Assipattle got on his back and patted his right shoulder he started off with a loud neigh. The noise wakened the father, who sprang up and called his sons. All of them mounted the best horses they could find and set out in pursuit of the thief, little knowing that it was Assipattle.

The father, who rode fastest almost overtook Teetgong, and he shouted to him,

> 'Hi, hi, ho!
> Teetgong wo!'

At that, Teetgong came at once to a halt. Assipattle put the goose thrapple to his mouth and blew as hard as he could. When Teetgong heard the sound he galloped away like the wind, leaving his master and the six sons far behind. The speed was such that Assipattle could hardly breathe.

It was almost dawn when Assipattle reached the coast where the Stoor Worm was lying. There was a dale between hills. In the dale was a small croft house. Assipattle tethered his horse and slipped into the croft. An old woman lay in bed, snoring loudly. The fire had been rested [banked up] and an iron pot stood beside it. Assipattle seized the pot. In it he placed a glowing peat from the fire. The old woman did not waken as he crept quietly out of her house, but the grey cat which lay at the bottom of her bed yawned and stretched itself.

Down to the shore Assipattle hurried. Far out from the land was a dark high island, which was really the top of the Stoor Worm's head. But close to the shore a boat was rocking at anchor. A man stood up in the boat swinging his arms across his chest, for it was a cold morning. Assipattle shouted to the man, 'Why don't you come on shore to warm yourself?'

'I would if I could,' replied the man, 'but the king's kamperman [seneschal] would beat me black and blue if I left the boat.'

'You had better stay then,' said Assipattle. 'As for myself, I am going to light a fire to cook limpets for my breakfast.' And he began to dig a hollow in the ground for a fireplace.

He dug for a minute or two, then he jumped up crying 'Gold! It must be gold! It's yellower than the corn and brighter than the sun!'

When the man in the boat heard this he jumped into the water and waded ashore. He almost knocked Assipattle down, so anxious was he to see the gold. With his bare hands he scratched the earth where Assipattle had been digging.

Meanwhile, Assipattle untied the painter and sprang into the boat with the pot in his hand. He was well out to sea when the man looked up from his digging and began to roar with rage. The sun appeared like a red ball over the end of the valley as Assipattle hoisted his sail and steered towards the head of the monster. When he looked behind, he could see that the king and all his men had gathered on the shore. Some of them were dancing with fury, bawling at him to come back. He paid no heed, knowing he must reach the Stoor Worm before the creature gave its seventh yawn.

The Stoor Worm's head was like a mountain and his eyes like round lochs, very dark and deep. When the sun shone in his eyes the monster wakened and began to yawn. He always gave seven long yawns, then his dreadful forked tongue shot out and seized any living thing that happened to be near. Assipattle steered close to the monster's mouth as he yawned a second time. With each yawn a vast tide of water was swept down the Stoor Worm's gullet. Assipattle and his boat were carried with it into the mighty cavern of the mouth, then down the throat, then along twisting passages like tremendous tunnels. Mile after mile he was whirled, with the water gurgling around him. At last the force of the current grew less, the water got shallower, and the boat grounded.

Assipattle knew that he had only a short time before the next yawn, so he ran, as he had never run in his life, round one corner after another until he came to the Stoor Worm's liver. He could see what he was about because all the inside of the monster was lit up by meeracles [phosphorescence].

He pulled out a muckle ragger [large knife] and cut a hole in the liver. Then he took the peat out of the pail and pushed it into the hole, blowing for all he was worth to make it burst into flame. He thought the fire would never take, and had almost given up hope, when there was a tremendous blaze and the liver began to burn and splutter like a Johnsmas bonfire. When he was sure that the whole liver would soon be burning, Assipattle ran back to his boat. He ran even faster than he had before, and he reached it just in time, for the burning liver made the Stoor Worm so ill that he retched and retched. A flood of water from the stomach caught the boat and carried it up to the monster's throat, and out of his mouth, and right to the shore, where it landed high and dry.

Although Assipattle was safe and sound, no one had any thought for him, for it seemed that the end of the world had come. The king and his men, and Assipattle, and the man who had been in the boat, and the old woman, who had been wakened by the noise, and the cat, all scrambled up the hill to escape from the floods that rushed from the Stoor Worm's mouth.

Bigger and bigger grew the fire. Black clouds of smoke swirled from the monster's nostrils, so that the sky was filled with darkness. In his agony he shot out his forked tongue until it laid hold of the horn of the moon. But it slipped off and fell back to earth with such an impact that it made a deep rift in the earth. The tide rushed into the rift, between the Danes' land and Norway. The place where the end of the tongue fell is the Baltic Sea. The Stoor Worm twisted and turned in torment. He flung his head up to the sky, and every time it fell the whole world shook and groaned. With each fall, teeth dropped out of the vile spewing mouth. The first lot became the Orkney Islands; the next lot became the Shetland Islands; and the last of all, when the Stoor Worm was almost dead, the Faroe Islands fell with an almighty splash into the sea. In the end the monster coiled itself tightly together into a huge mass. Old folk say the far country of Iceland is the dead body of the Stoor Worm, with the liver still blazing beneath its burning mountains.

After a long while the sky cleared and the sun shone, and the people came to themselves again. The king took Assipattle into his arms and called him his son. He dressed Assipattle in a crimson robe, and put the fair white hand of Gem-de-Lovely into the hand of Assipattle. Then he girded the sword Snikkersnapper onto Assipattle. And he said that as far as his kingdom stretched, north, south, east and west, everything belonged to the hero who had saved the land and people.

A week later, Assipattle and Gem-de-Lovely were married in the royal palace. Never was there such a wedding, for everyone in the kingdom was happy that the Stoor Worm would never trouble them again. All over the country there was singing and dancing. King Assipattle and Queen Gem-de-Lovely were full of joy, for they loved each other so much. They had ever so many fine bairns; and if they are not dead, they are living yet.

E. W. Marwick, *The Folklore of Orkney and Shetland*,
Batsford 1974, 139–44

# Gazetteer of Places with Dragon Legends

*(with National Grid references)*

ENGLAND

**Buckinghamshire**
Hughenden   SU89

**Cheshire**
Moston   SJ 66

**Derbyshire**
Drakelow   SK 21

**Devon**
Cadbury Castle/Dolbury Hill
    SS 90
Challacombe   SS 64
Manaton   SX 78
Winkleigh   SS 60

**Durham**
Lambton Castle, near Chester-le-
    Street   NZ 25
Sockburn   NZ 30
Bishop Auckland   NZ 22

**Essex**
Henham   TL 52
Hornden   TQ 68
St Osyth   TM 11
Saffron Walden (cockatrice)
    TL 53
Wormingford   TL 93

**Gloucestershire**
Deerhurst   SO 32
Stinchcombe   ST 79

**Hampshire**
Bisterne   SU 10
Wherwell (cockatrice)   SU 34

**Hereford and Worcester**
Brinsop   SO 44
Wormelow Tump   SO 43

**Hertfordshire**
Brent Pelham   TL 43
St Albans   TL 10

**Lincolnshire**
Anwick   TF 15
Castle Carlton   TF 38
Walmsgate   TF 37

**Norfolk**
Ludham   TG 31

**Northumberland**
Bamburgh   NU 13
Money Hill (on Gunnarton
    Fell)   NZ 97
Longwitton NZ 08

**Oxfordshire**
Dragonhoard (near Garsington)
    SP 50
White Horse Hill, near Uffington,
    formerly Berkshire   SU 38

**Shropshire**
Old Field Barrows, near Bromfield
    SO 47

*Somerset*
Aller    ST 42
Carhampton    ST 04
Castle Neroche, near Ilminster
    ST 31
Churchstanton    ST 11
Crowcombe    ST 13
Kilve    ST 14
Kingston St Mary    ST 22
Norton Fitzwarren    ST 12
Shervage Wood    ST 13
*Suffolk*
Bures    TL 93
Little Cornard    TL 92
*Sussex (West)*
Bignor Hill    SU 91
Lyminster    TQ 00
St Leonard's Forest    TQ 23
*Worcestershire*
Drakelowe, near Wolverley    SO 87
*Yorkshire (North)*
Beckhole
Drake Howe, Bilsdale    NZ 50
Filey Brigg    TA 18
Handale Priory, near Lofthouse
    SE 07
Kellington    SE 52
Nunnington    SE 67
Sexhow    NZ 40
Slingsby    SE 67
Well    SE 28
*Yorkshire (South)*
Wantley, near Wortley    SK 39

WALES
*Clwyd*
Llanrhaeadr-ym-Mochnant,
    formerly in Denbighshire SJ 12
*Dyfed*
Newcastle Emlyn, formerly in
    Carmarthen    SN 34

Wiston, formerly in Pembroke
    (cockatrice)    SN 01
*Glamorgan (South)*
Penllin Castle    SS 97
Penmark    ST 06
*Gwynedd*
Llyn Cynwch, near Dolgellau,
    formerly in Merioneth    SH 72
Llyn-y-Gader, formerly in
    Caernarvon    SH 55
Penmynydd, formerly in
    Angelsey    SH 57
*Powys*
Llandeilo Graban, formerly in
    Breconshire    SN 04

SCOTLAND
*Borders*
Linton, formerly in Roxburgh
    NT 72
*Dumfries and Galloway*
Dalry, formerly in Kirkcudbright
    NX 68
*Highlands*
Ben Vair, formerly in
    Inverness    NN 06
Cnoc-na-Cnoimh, in Glen Cassley,
    formerly in Sutherland
    NC 41
*Tayside*
Strathmartin, formerly in Angus
    NO 33

ORKNEY ISLANDS
No specific location mentioned for
the fight with the Stoor Worm.

CHANNEL ISLES
*Jersey*
La Hougue Bie, near Five Oaks

# Dates Relevant to British Dragon Legends (Pre-1800)

| | |
|---|---|
| c.1120 | The Abbot of St Albans flattens the 'dragon's cave' at Wormenhert |
| c.1130 | A capital in Reading Abbey shows men fighting dragons |
| c.1150 | Tympanum on Brinsop Church showing St George and Dragon |
| c.1250 | Tombstone in Lyminster churchyard, later said to be of dragon-slayer |
| c.1310 | Conyers tomb in Sockburn Church, later said to be of dragon-slayer |
| c.1325 | Tomb in Nunnington Church, later said to be of dragon-slayer |
| 1389 | Guild of St George founded in Norwich |
| 1396 | First mention of Conyers falchion ceremony |
| 1399 | First mention of Pollard falchion ceremony |
| 1405 | Henry de Blaneford's *Chronicle* mentions Bures dragon |
| 1408 | First mention of Snap of Norwich in religious pageant |
| 1456 | Play about St George at Lydd, with dragon figure |
| 1491 | Dragon-images mentioned at St Margaret's Church, Westminster |
| c.1500 | Rood-screen at Norton Fitzwarren church, showing dragon-fight |
| 1502 | Dragon-images mentioned again at St Margaret's, Westminster |
| 1511 | Play about St George at Bassingbourn, with dragon |
| 1519 | Procession with dragon-image at Wymondham |
| 1539–1614 | Incumbency of the Vicar of Brent Pelham who first recorded the story of Piers Shonks and the dragon |
| 1558 | Snap of Norwich mentioned in civic pageant. |
| 1583 | Phillip Stubbes, *Anatomie of Abuses*: describes dragon- |

figures accompanying Morris dancers in procession to a church

1586 William Camden's *Britannia*: mentions the Burford processional dragon-image, and the legends of dragon-slaying at Sockburn and Castle Carlton

1608 Edward Topsell, *The Historie of Serpents*

1614 Chapbook on the dragon in St Leonard's Forest

1619 Dragon-slaying legend at Slingsby mentioned by Roger Dodsworth

1630 T. Risdon, A *Survey of Devon*, mentions dragon of Cadbury Castle and Dolbury Hill, and Thomas Westcote, A *View of Devonshire*, mentions those at Challacombe

1636 William Sampson's *The Vow Breaker* alludes to a dragon-image, hobby-horse, St George and Morris dancers

1660–70 First two mentions of dragon painting on Mordiford Church

1669 Chapbook on the Monstrous Serpent at Henham

1674 Fair at Henham selling 'flying serpents'

1680 Linton dragon mentioned in *The History of the Somervilles*

1685 Broadside ballad, *A True Relation of the Dreadful Combat between More of More Hall and the Dragon of Wantley*

1704 Broadside referring to the dragon at St Osyth's in Henry II's reign

1712 Robert Atkyns *The Ancient and Present State of Gloucester-shire* mentions the dragon-slaying legend at Deerhurst

1734 Falle, *History of Jersey*, mentions Hambye dragon-slaying legend

1737 Henry Carey's burlesque opera 'The Dragon of Wantley'

1738 Francis Wise, A *Letter to Dr Meade*, mentions legend of St George and the dragon associated with the White Horse of Uffington

c.1750 Two London taverns named 'The Essex Serpent' in allusion to the serpent of Henham.

1758 Letter referring to the Hughenden dragon in the October issue of *The Gentleman's Magazine*

1772 Mock-guild founded at Pockthorpe, Norwich, with its own Snap

1779 Mummers' Play at Revesby included a dragon ('worm') in performance

1793 *The Statistical Account of Scotland* mentions dragon-slaying legend at Strathmartin, and also sightings of 'fiery dragons' in sky

# Notes

The titles and dates of books and articles frequently cited will be given in full on the first occasion that they are mentioned, but thereafter will be referred to by the author's name only. Full details can also be found in the Bibliography.

## Chapter One – The Background: Dragons Down the Ages

1 Prehistoric Reptiles. E. S. Hartland, *The Legend of Perseus*, 1896, III, 66–7.

2 Fossils displayed as Dragons. E. E. Ploss, *Siegfried-Sigurd der Drachen-kämpfer*, 1966, 56n, 160; Richard Carrington, *Mermaids and Mastodons*, Chatto and Windus, 1957, 71; P. Costello, *In Search of Lake Monsters*, 1974, 314.

3 The Stronsay Bones. *Transactions of the Wernerian Natural History Society* I, 1811, 418ff.; illustration from this reproduced in Carrington, 26. See also E. Marwick, *The Folklore of Orkney and Shetland*, 1974, 22, 185.

4 The Newcastle Fish. See J. B. Sweeney, *A Pictorial History of Sea Monsters*, 1972, 85. The allusion to 'the captain of the *Daedalus*' in the newspaper report refers to a celebrated incident in 1848 when a Sea Serpent was sighted by this ship.

5 Indra and Vṛtra. *Rg Veda* I.32.1–15, translated by Wendy D. O'Flaherty, *Hindu Myths*, Penguin, 1975, 74–6; the later version of this myth, *Mâhabhârata* 5.9, 5.10, and 5.13, is translated in the same work, 76–84.

6 Marduk and Tiamat. Extracts from *Enuma Elish*, translated by E. A. Speiser in *Ancient Near Eastern Texts Relating to the Old Testament*, ed. J. B. Pritchard, 1955. See also John Gray, *Near Eastern Mythology*, 1969.

7 Yahweh and Leviathan. See T. H. Gaster, *Thespes: Ritual, Myth and Drama in the Ancient Near East*, 1950, 73–97, 145–50; J. Fontenrose, *Python*, 1959, 209–10.

8 Snake Moneyboxes. M. P. Nilsson, 'Draken pa skatten,' *Folkminner och Folktenkar* XXIX, 1942, 81–5.

9 'The Dragon Slayer' Fairytale. Well over 1000 examples are known; it is classified as AT 300 in Antti Aarne and Stith Thompson, *The Types of the Folktale*, 1961, and also occurs as an inset episode in AT 303, 'The Two Brothers'. The basic study of this tale is Kurt Ranke, *Die Zwei Brüder*, 1934; his findings are summarised and assessed in Stith Thompson, *The Folktale*, 1946 (reprint 1977), 22–32.

10 Dragon Standards. Rodney Dennys, *The Heraldic Imagination*, 1975, 186–92. The reference to their use in Roman triumphs is in Ammianus Marcellinus XVI, 10.7.

11 Faked Dragons. Carrington, 69–70, including reproductions of probable examples from the illustrations of Ulisse Aldroyandi: see also Sweeney, 37.

## Chapter Two – Habits and Habitats of British Dragons

1 Beowulf's Dragon. *Beowulf* lines 2270–77, 2824–35, transl. J. Simpson.

2 Barrows. For those at Garsington, Wolverley, Old Field Barrows (Salop), Drakelow (Derbyshire), Walmsgate, and Drake Howe (North Yorks.), see L. V. Grinsell, *The Folklore of Prehistoric Sites in Britain*, 1976, 145, 154, 156, 158, 161, 172–3, and references there given; for Trellech, see Marie Trevelyan, *Folk-Lore and Folk Stories of Wales*, 1909, 167–8; for Wormelow Tump, H. Bett, *English Legends*, 1950, 98; for Money Hill on Gunnarton Fell, Janet Bord and Colin Bord, *The Secret Country*, 1977.

3 Drake Stones. At Stinchcombe, Grinsell 141; at Anwick, E. H. Rudkin, *Lincolnshire Folklore*, 1936, 56–7.

4 Exe Valley. Theo Brown, 'The Folklore of Devon,' *Folklore* LXXV, 1964, 147; T. Risdon, A *Survey of Devon*, c.1630, reprinted 1970, 78. (In the rhyme, 'eare' means 'to plough', and 'share' a ploughshare).

5 Cissbury Snakes. C. Latham, 'Some West Sussex Superstitions Lingering in 1868,' *Folk-Lore Record* I, 1878, 16–17.

6 Welsh Snakes. Trevelyan, 173–4.

7 Destructive Dragons. In the Orkneys, Marwick 139; at Lyminster in Sussex, S. G. Joiner, 'The Knucker of Lyminster,' *Sussex County Magazine* III, 1929, 845; at Moston in Cheshire, E. Leigh, *Ballads and Legends of Cheshire*, 1866, 223–7.

8 Nine Maidens' Well, Strathmartin. Robert Chambers, *The Book of Days*, 1864, I, 541; *The Statistical Account of Scotland*, 1793, as cited in John

Brand, *Popular Antiquities of Great Britain*, revised by Sir Henry Ellis, 1853 ed., I, 322.

9 Longwitton. F. Grice, *Folktales of the North Country*, 1944, 95; see also John Hodgson, A *History of Northumberland*, 1827–1840, Part II vol. III, 308–9, note (quoted in M. C. Balfour, *County Folklore IV: Northumberland*, 1904, 5.)

10 Lambton Worm. Anon., *The Wonderful History of the Lambton Worm*, n.d. (*c.*1875), reprint 1968; anon. folksong, 'The Lambton Worm'. Both printed in Appendix A above, pp. 124–9. See also William Henderson, *Notes on the Folklore of the Northern Counties of England and The Borders*, 1879 (reprint 1973), 247–53; his version is based on stories gathered *c.*1830.

11 Flying Dragons. In Wales, Trevelyan 168–9; in Devon, Brown, 149. In Essex, see A. Adshead, 'The Flying Serpent of Henham', *Essex Countryside*, Autumn 1954. The pubs named from this episode are in King Street, Covent Garden, and Charles Street, Westminster; they date from about 1750. I am grateful to A. W. Smith for these Essex and London references.

12 Dragon of Castle Carlton. Christopher Marlowe, *Legends of the Fenland People*, 1926 (reprinted by EP Publishing, 1976), 57–8.

13 Dangerous breath of Snakes. Quotations taken from Ramona and Desmond Morris, *Men and Snakes*, 1965, 123.

14 Women's Milk causes Dragons. Elias Owen, *Welsh Folklore*, 1896 (reprinted 1976), 349; Sir John Rhys, *Celtic Folklore*, 1901, II, 690.

15 Infancy of Dragons. J. Dacres Devlin, *The Mordiford Dragon*, 1848 (reprinted 1978), 6–13; *Wonderful Legend of the Lambton Worm*, 4.

16 Newts at Mordiford. H. J. Massingham, *The Southern Marches*, 1952, 256–8; this jest is classified in the Aarne-Thompson system as AT 1310, 'Drowning the Crayfish as Punishment'.

17 Cockatrice at Saffron Walden. A. Lyons, 'Essex Dragons,' *Essex Countryside*, Summer 1956.

18 Cockatrice at Wherwell. Wendy Boase, *Folklore in Hampshire and the Isle of Wight*, Batsford, 1976, 110, citing W. G. Beddington and E. B. Christie, *It Happened in Hampshire*, 1937, 115–16.

19 Distribution of Dragons. Henderson, 260.

20 Wyvern of Llyn Cynwch. B. Henderson and S. Jones, *Wonder Tales of Ancient Wales*, 1921, cited in F. W. Holiday, *The Dragon and the Disc*, 1973, 85–6.

21 Water Snakes. At Cardiff, Trevelyan, 9, 14; in Ireland, Lady Gregory, *Visions and Beliefs in the West of Ireland*, 1920 (paperback edition

1976), 280; in the River Ness, Adamnan's *Life of St Columba* (*c.*670), transl. William Reeves, 1856. Further Scottish water-snakes are mentioned in R. Macdonald Robertson, *Selected Highland Folk Tales*, 1961 (reprint 1977), 122–9.

22 The Flood at Mordiford. Devlin, 24–5.

23 The Dragon at Dalry. Andrew Lang, in *Academy*, October 17, 1885; Lang's correction of the location is noted by E. S. Hartland, *The Antiquary* XXXVIII, 1902, 4, footnote.

24 Dragon on Church Tower. D. Edmondes Owen, 'Pre-Reformation Survivals', *Transactions of the Honourable Society of Cymmrodorion*, 1910–11, as quoted by W. H. Howse, *Radnorshire*, 1949, 201.

25 Jim Pulk and the Knucker. Personal letter from Rosemary Anne Sisson to Jacqueline Simpson, December 1971, from a tale told to her by a gardener in Lyminster in the 1930s.

## Chapter Three – The Hero: Knight or Churl?

1 St George at Brinsop. E. M. Leather, *The Folk-Lore of Herefordshire*, 1912, 11.

2 St George at Uffington. Stuart Piggott, *Antiquity* V, 1931, 44–5; M. Marples, *White Horses and Other Hill Figures*, 1949, 50; D. Woolner, 'New Light on the White Horse', *Folklore* LXXVIII, 1967, 90–112, especially 102; the legend was first mentioned by Francis Wise in 1738.

3 St Leonard. M. A. Lower, 'Old Speech and Old Manners in Sussex', *Sussex Archaeological Collections* XIII, 1861, 223–5; on the place-name 'Dragon's Green', see Jill Glover, *The Place-names of Sussex*, 1975, 48.

4 St Carantoc and St Petroc. C. Horstman, *Nova Legenda Angliae*, 1901, I, 178–9, II, 318–19 (transl. J. Simpson.)

5 Fulke Fitzwarrin. This summary of the medieval romance is from Maurice Keen, *The Outlaws of Medieval Legend*, Routledge and Kegan Paul, 1961, 43; the modern legend from Norton Fitzwarren is in Kingsley Palmer, *The Folklore of Somerset*, 1976, 77–8.

6 Sir Guy of Warwick. John Hodgson, *A History of Northumberland*, 1827–40, Part II vol. III, 308–9, note.

7 The Laidly Worm. Text of 'Kemp Owyne' from A. Quiller-Couch, *The Oxford Book of Ballads*, 1910, no. 13; the legend of Spindlestone Heugh, together with the verses by the Rev. Mr Lamb, are in Henderson, 254–6. See also F. J. Child, *English and Scottish Popular Ballads*, 1957 ed., I, 311–13.

8 The Sockburn Worm. Henderson, 245–6; C. R. Beard, *Lucks and Talismans*, n.d., 227, citing William Camden, *Britannia*, 1586, II, 132.

9  The Pollard Worm (Brawn). Henderson, 246–7; Beard, 228.

10  The Linton Dragon. Henderson, 256-8; G. F. Leishman, *Linton Leaves*, 1937, 10–11, citing *The Memoirs of the Somervilles*, 1680.

11  The Bisterne Dragon. D. Goldring, *Nooks and Corners of Sussex and Hampshire*, n.d. (c.1925), 233.

12  The Dragon of Well. E. Bogg, *From Eden Vale to the Plains of York*, n.d., cited in E. Gutch, *Country Folklore II: North Riding of Yorkshire*, 1899 (reprint 1967), 81.

13  The Dragon of Castle Carlton. Camden, p. 384 cols. I and II, additions; cited in E. Gutch and M. C. Peacock, *County Folklore V: Lincolnshire*, 1908, 34. Modern version, Marlowe 60–1.

14  Sir John Lambton. Robert Surtees, *The History and Antiquities of the County Palatine of Durham*, 1820, II, 171. The Lambton legend and that of Deodat de Gozon are both discussed by J.A. Boyle, 'Historical Dragon Slayers', in *Animals in Folklore*, ed. J. R. Porter and W. M. S. Russell, 1978, 26–7, but this author does not suggest a cause-and-effect connexion between them.

15  Piers Shonks. Doris Jones-Baker, *The Folklore of Hertfordshire*, Batsford 1977, 49–50.

16  The Garstons of Mordiford. Devlin, 14–15, 32.

17  Smith of Deerhurst. Hartland, 1902, 1–6, citing R. Atkyns, *The Ancient and Present State of Gloucestershire*, 2nd ed. 1768, 202; see also S. Rudder, *A New History of Gloucestershire*, 1779, 402.

18  The Bures Dragon. Translated from Henry de Blaneford's continuation of the *Chronicle* of John de Trokelow (ed. H. G. Riley, Rolls Series, 1866, IV); cited in Winifred Beaumont, *Wormingford: A Short History of the Church and Parish*, 1957, 12.

19  John Aller. Berta Lawrence, *Somerset Legends*, 1973, 95–6. See also T. W. Higgins, 'John Aller,' *Folklore* IV, 1893, 399–400; Palmer, 79. In Berta Lawrence's account, the phrase 'The Dragon of Aller was slain by a harrow' looks as if it is in fact a couplet of verse, similar to many local folk-rhymes, with 'harrow' pronounced dialectally as 'harrer'.

20  Hector Gunn. Robertson, 1961, 130–1.

21  The Blacksmith of Dalry. Hartland, 1896, III, 87–8.

22  The Criminal at Mordiford. Devlin, 17–23; Leather, 24; Massingham, 256–8.

23  Death of John Aller. Higgins, 399–400.

24  The Bisterne Dragon. Boase, 110–111. See also Beddington and Christie, 116; L. Collinson-Morley, *Companion into Hampshire*, 1948, 231; F. E. Stevens, *Hampshire Ways*, 1934, 125–6 (all cited by Boase).

25 Sir Peter Loschy. H. L. Gee, *Folk Tales of Yorkshire*, 1952, 123–5.

26 Wyvill of Slingsby. *The Leisure Hour*, 4 May 1878, 279, cited in Gutch, 81. Mrs Gutch states that the legend was first noted by the antiquarian Roger Dodsworth in 1619.

27 The Seigneur de Hambye. J. H. L'Amy, *Jersey Folk Lore*, 1927 (reprint 1971), 37–8, citing Falle's *History of Jersey*, 1734. Hambye is in Normandy, but the Paisnel family, whose seat it was, in the thirteenth century owned the estate in Jersey where the dragon is said to have been slain; a mound called La Hougue Bie, allegedly marking the knight's grave, is in fact prehistoric.

28 The Curse on the Lambtons. Henderson, 247–53; *Wonderful Legend*, Appendix A, 126.

29 Fated Death at Penmynedd. T. Gwyn Jones, *Welsh Folklore and Folk Custom*, 1930 (reprint 1979), 85.

## Chapter Four – The Tactics of Draconicide

1 Dragon of Castle Carlton. Marlowe, 59–60.

2 The Dragon of Longwitton. Grice, 95–6; Hodgson, 308–9, notes, for the older version.

3 The Dragon of Ludham. Enid Porter, *The Folklore of East Anglia*, 1974, 130.

4 The Dragons of Ben Vair. Robertson, 141.

5 The Worm of Shervage Wood. C.W. Whistler, 'Local Traditions in the Quantocks', *Folklore* XIX, 1908, 35; see also Ruth Tongue, *Somerset Folklore*, 1965, 130–1.

6 The Dragon of Kingston St Mary. Tongue, 129–30, from local informants in 1911.

7 The Dragon of Bisterne. Goldring, 233.

8 The Dragon of Penymnedd. T. Gwyn Jones, 85.

9 The Cockatrice of Castle Gwys. Trevelyan, 177.

10 Spiked Armour. For the Lambton story, see Henderson, 247–53, and *Wonderful Legend*, Sir Cuthbert Sharp, 1830 and 1834; also for the Dragon of Wantley, pages 135–6; for the story from Dalry, see Andrew Lang in *The Academy*, 17 October 1885, and Hartland, 1896, III, 87–8.

11 Hedgehogs and Vipers. Morris and Morris, 185.

12 Spiked Barrels. At Mordiford, Devlin, 17–23; at Ben Vair, Robertson, 140–1.

13 Spiked Pillar. Trevelyan, 167.

14 Spiked Dummy. D. E. Owen, quoted by Howse, 201.

15 Wyvern at Newcastle Emlyn. Janet Bord and Colin Bord, *The Secret Country*, 1977, 76.

16 The Dragon of Filey Brigg. Ruth Tongue, 'Billy Biter and the Parkin', *Folklore* LXXVIII, 1967, 139–41.

17 Jim Puttock and the Knucker. Joiner, 846–7 (see above, pages 130–2).

18 The Worm of Cnoc-Na-Cnoimh. Robertson, 131–2.

19 Assipattle and the Stoor Worm. Marwick, 143, based on oral traditions and on nineteenth-century versions compiled by Walter Traill Dennison.

## Chapter Five – 'You Can See It There Still'

1 Tomb of Piers Shonks as Proof. Comment recorded by H. W. Tomkyns in *Highways and Byways in Hertfordshire*, 1902, and cited in Jones-Baker, 60.

2 The Dragon of Wantley. The topographical information was supplied to Bishop Thomas Percy in 1767, and published by him as a note to the poem in the fourth edition of his *Reliques of Ancient English Poetry*, 1794 (Everyman Edition, 1906, II, 376–7.) The poem itself was also included in the 1699 edition of *Wit and Mirth: Or Pills to Purge Melancholy*, but without any topographical comments.

3 Coffin at Handale Priory. J. W. Ord, *The History and Antiquities of Cleveland*, 1846, 282–3; cited in Gutch, 77–8.

4 Coffin Cover at Kellington. T. Parkinson, *Yorkshire Legends and Traditions*, 1889, II, 238.

5 Lyminster Tombstone. Personal observation.

6 Piers Shonks and his Tomb. Jones-Baker, 60–1; see also Betty Puttick, 'The Hertfordshire St George and the Dragon', *Hertfordshire Countryside*, March 1966, 311.

7 Painted Dragon at Mordiford. John Aubrey, *The Natural Historie of Wiltshire*, I, Bodleian MS Aubrey I, 132v., quoted by M. Hunter, *John Aubrey and the Realm of Learning*, 1975, 227. See also Devlin, 14–15, 17, 36, 40–2, 66, 69–70; also Leather, 24. For the dragon-image of uncertain provenance, see C. Dingley, *History from Marble*, Camden Society 1867–8, I, cciv, 102; I am grateful to Mrs Ellen Ettlinger for tracking down this reference, and for her suggestion that the object represented might be a weathervane.

8 Carved Bench at Crowcombe. Whistler, 35.

9 Dragon Relics. At Lambton Castle, Henderson, 252; at Sexhow, *The Leisure Hour*, 4 May 1878, cited by Gutch, 80; at Arundel, J. Larwood and J. C. Hotton, *English Inn Signs*, 1951 (a revised edition of a work

published in 1886 as *The History of Signboards*), 102; at Taunton Museum, Readers' Digest *Folklore* etc, 159. Dr K. P. Oakley kindly informs me (18.10.1978) that he knows of no instance of fossils being claimed as dragon bones in the British Isles.

10 Wormingford. When quoting the Bures legend, Winifred Beaumont (*Wormingford: A Short History of the Church and Parish*, 12) entitles her account 'The Legend of the Wormingford Dragon'. For the earlier forms of the place name, see Morant, *The History and Antiquities of the County of Essex*, 1768, II, 231; I am grateful to Doris Jones-Baker for this information.

## Chapter Six – Dragons in Plays and Pageants

1 Snap. Most of the information on Snap throughout this chapter is derived from Richard Lane, *Snap the Norwich Dragon*, 1976. Further details can be found in Porter, 61–3, and in E. C. Cawte, *Ritual Animal Disguise*, 1978, 36–9.

2 The Lord of Misrule's Procession. Philip Stubbes, *The Anatomie of Abuses*, 1583, fol. 92; cited in Brand, I, 501–2, and Cawte, 45.

3 Snap's Esteemed Position. Lane, 5.

4 Rogation Day Dragons. Chambers, I, 541; the theory was taken up again in an article by Alison Ross, 'Cakes and Ale for the Dragon Slayers', *The Times*, 2 June 1973, but with no additional evidence. See W. Hone, *Ancient Mysteries Described*, 1823, 134; I am grateful to Miss Christina Hole for confirming my impression that the theory has no basis in British customs.

5 St George Procession at Norwich. Lane, 21–2.

6 Other Church Plays and Processions. At Bassingbourn, Jones-Baker, 58; at Westminster, *Illustrations of the Manners and Expenses of Ancient Times in England*, 1797, as cited in Brand I, 322–3; at Wymondham, Wigtoft, Heybridge, Walberswick and Leicester, Cawte 38–9, and references there given.

7 Chester Pageant. J. Hemingway, *A History of the City of Chester*, 1831, I, 201–4; Chambers, I, 236–7; Cawte, 29.

8 Midsummer Pageant at Burford. K. M. Briggs, *The Folklore of the Cotswolds*, 1974, 28.

9 'The Vow Breaker'. Quoted in Brand, I, 197.

10 Burford Mummers' Play. Briggs, 187–90.

11 The Revesby Play. Quoted in Brand, I, 513; see also Cawte, 80–1.

12 The Costessey Snap. Porter, 63–5.

13 The Pockthorpe Snap. Lane, 29.

14 The Minehead Horse as 'Sea Serpent'. Readers' Digest, *Folklore* etc., 160.

15 St George at Padstow. M. A. Courtney, *Cornish Feasts and Folklore*, 1890, 32.

16 The May Dragon in the River Stour. Personal information from Mrs Doris Jones-Baker, who collected the tale from oral informants in the area in 1976.

17 Capital from Reading Abbey. Ellen Ettlinger, 'A Romanesque Capital from Reading Abbey in the Reading Museum and Art Gallery', *Berkshire Archaeological Journal* LXVIII, 1977, 71–5.

## Chapter Seven – Problems, Theories and Conclusions

1 Coyote and the Water Monster. E. E. Clark, *Indian Legends of the Pacific North-West*, 1953, 89–91.

2 Isfadiar and the Dragon. Quoted in E. Ingersoll, *Dragons and Dragon Lore*, 1928, 40–1.

3 The Knucker's Sneeze. G. B. Stuart, 'The Dragon's Pool', *Sussex County Magazine* VI, 1932, 154–6.

4 The Cave at Wormenhert. Jones-Baker, 55, citing Matthew Paris, *Gesta Abbatium Monasticii Sancti Albani*.

5 Heraldry. A. C. Fox-Davies, A *Complete Guide to Heraldry*, 1909, 326–7; Rodney Dennys, *The Heraldic Imagination*, 1975, 190–1.

6 The Dragon of St Leonard's forest. *True and Wonderful: A Discourse Relating a Strange and Monstrous Serpent (or Dragon) . . . this present Month of August 1614*, in *The Harleian Miscellany, 1745*, III, 106–9; the full text may be read in E. V. Lucas, *Highways and Byways of Sussex*, 1904, and in J. Simpson, *The Folklore of Sussex*, 1973, 35–6. The notoriety of this pamphlet, and the mockery it aroused, are seen in references in Jonson's 'World in the Moon' and Beaumont and Fletcher's 'Wit Without Money', and also in the anonymous *Ballet of the Manner of the killing of the Serpent in Sussex*, September 1614; see H. R. Rollins, *An Analytical Index to the Ballad Entries (1557–1709) in the Registers of the Company of Stationers In London*, 1967, 144. The Hornden Serpent. Lyons.

7 Flying Dragons at Aberdeen. A *Statistical Account of Scotland*, 1793, VI, 467.

8 Occult Theories. Examples of this way of thought include F. W. Holiday, *The Dragon and the Disc*, 1973; Francis Hitching, *Earth Magic*, 1976; Janet Bord and Colin Bord, *Mysterious Britain*, 1974, and *The Secret Country*, 1977; Paul Screeton, *The Lambton Worm and Other Northumbrian Dragon Legends*, 1978.

9 The Fighting Dragons of Little Cornard. Readers' Digest, *Folklore*, etc, 241.

10 Wormingford Church Window. Beaumont, 12.

11 Lawsuit at Wantley. Percy, II, 377–8; the interpretation was given him by Godfrey Bosville, Esq., of Thorp, near Malton (Yorkshire), a descendent of one of the persons involved in the lawsuit. See also Llewellyn Jewitt, *The Dragon of Wantley and the family of More*, London, 1887; David, Hey, 'The Dragon of Wantley', *Rural History*, 4:1, 1933, 23–40.

12 The Boar of Brancepeth. Grice, 94–5.

13 Psychological Interpretation. According to Jung, the perfect form of dragon-tale is one in which the hero is swallowed by a water-monster, destroys it from within, and escapes alive; it symbolises the destruction of the Mother in her terrifying aspects, from within the womb, and the consequent rebirth of the hero. See C. G. Jung, *Symbols of Transformation* (transl. R. F. C. Hull), 1956. The 'racial memory of dinosaurs' theory has recently been revived by Carl Sagan in *The Dragons of Eden: Speculations on the Evolution of Human Intelligence*, London and New York, 1978.

14 Sigurd's Trick. Ploss, 33–4.

# Select Bibliography

The following are the chief works consulted; others, from which only minor or occasional items have been taken, will be found in the Notes under the relevant heading.

Adamnan, *The Life of St Columba*, transl. by W. Reeves, 1856

Adshead, A., 'The Flying Serpent of Henham', *Essex Countryside*, Autumn 1954

Atkyns, R., *The Ancient and Present State of Gloucester*, 1768

Balfour, M. C., *County Folk-Lore IV: Northumberland*, 1904

Beard, C. R., *Lucks and Talismans*, n.d.

Beaumont, W., *Wormingford: A Short History of the Church and Parish*, 1957

Beddington, W. G., and Christy, E. B., *It Happened in Hampshire*, 1937

Bett, E. H., *English Legends*, 1950

Boase, W., *The Folklore of Hampshire and the Isle of Wight*, 1976

Bogg, E., *From Eden Vale to the Plains of York*, n.d.

Boyle, J., 'Historical Dragon Slayers', in *Animals in Folklore*, ed. J. R. Porter and W. M. S. Russell, 1978, 23–32

Brand, J., *Observations of the Popular Antiquities of Great Britain*, revised and enlarged by Sir Henry Ellis, 1853

Briggs, K. M., *The Folklore of the Cotswolds*, 1974

Brown, T., 'The Folklore of Devon', *Folklore* LXXV, 1964, 145–60

Camden, W., *Britannia*, 1586

Carrington, R., *Mermaids and Mastodons*, 1957

Cawte, E. C., *Ritual Animal Disguise*, 1978

Chambers, R. W., *The Book of Days*, 1862–4

Courtney, M. A., *Cornish Feasts and Festivals*, 1890

Dennis, R., *The Heraldic Imagination*, 1975

Devlin, J. D., *The Mordiford Dragon*, 1848 (reprint 1978)

Dumont, L., *La Tarasque*, 1951

Ettlinger, E., 'A Romanesque Capital from Reading Abbey', *The Berkshire Archaeological Journal*, LXVIII, 1977, 71–5

Fontenrose, J., *Python*, 1959

Gee, H. L., *Folk Tales of Yorkshire*, 1952

Goldring, D., *Nooks and Corners of Sussex and Hampshire*, n.d. (*c.*1925)

Gregory, Lady, *Visions and Beliefs in the West of Ireland*, 1920 (reprint 1976)

Grice, F., *Folk Tales of the North Country*, 1944

Grinsell, L. V., *The Folklore of Prehistoric Sites in Britain*, 1976

Gutch, E., *County Folk-Lore II: North Riding of Yorkshire*, 1899

Gutch, E., and Balfour, M. C., *County Folk-Lore V: Lincolnshire*, 1908

Harper, Clive, *The Hughenden Dragon*, 1985

Hartland, E. S., 'The Dragon of Deerhurst', *The Antiquary* XXXVIII, 1902, 1–6

Hartland, E. S., *The Legend of Perseus*, 1896

Hemingway, J., *A History of the City of Chester*, 1831

Henderson, B., and Jones, S., *Wonder Tales of Ancient Wales*, 1921

Henderson, W., *Notes on the Folklore of the Northern Counties of England and the Border*, 1879 (reprint 1973)

Hey, David, 'The Dragon of Wantley: Rural Popular Culture and Local Legend', *Rural History: Economy, Society, Culture*, 4:1, 1993, 23–40

Higgins, T. W., 'John Aller', *Folklore* IV, 1893, 399–400

Hodgson, J., *A History of Northumberland*, 1827–1840

Hogarth, P., and Clery, V., *Dragons*, 1979

Horstman, C., *Nova Legenda Angliae*, 1901

Huxley, F., *The Dragon, Nature of Spirit, Spirit of Nature*, 1979

Howse, W. A., *Radnorshire*, 1949

Ingersoll, E., *Dragons and Dragon Lore*, 1928 (reprint Detroit 1968)

Joiner, S. C., 'The Knucker of Lyminster', *Sussex County Magazine* III, 1929, 845–6

Jones, T. Gwyn, *Welsh Folklore and Folk Custom*, 1930 (reprint 1979)

Jones-Baker, D., *The Folklore of Hertfordshire*, 1977

L'Amy, J. H., *Jersey Folk Lore*, 1927 (reprint 1971)

Lane, R., *Snap the Norwich Dragon*, 1976

Latham, C., 'Some West Sussex Superstitions Lingering in 1868', *Folk-Lore Record* I, 1878, 1–67

Lawrence, B., *Somerset Legends*, 1973

Leather, E. F., *The Folk-Lore of Herefordshire*, 1912

Leigh, E., *Ballads and Legends of Cheshire*, 1866

Leishman, G. F., *Linton Leaves*, 1937

Lower, M. A., 'Old Speech and Old Manners in Sussex', *Sussex Archaeological Collections* XIII, 1861, 209–36

Lyons, A., 'Essex Dragons', *Essex Countryside*, Summer 1956

Marlowe, C., *Legends of the Fenland People*, 1926 (reprint 1976)

Marples, M., *White Horses and Other Hill Figures*, 1949

Marwick, E., *The Folklore of Orkney and Shetland*, 1974

Massingham, H. J., *The Southern Marches*, 1952

Morris, R., and Morris, D., *Men and Snakes*, 1965

Ord, W. J., *The History and Antiquities of Cleveland*, 1846

Owen, D. E., 'Pre-Reformation Survivals', *Transactions of the Honourable Society of Cymmrodorion*, 1910–11

Owen, E., *Welsh Folk Lore*, 1896 (reprint 1976)

Palmer, K., *The Folklore of Somerset*, 1976

Parkinson, T., *Yorkshire Legends and Traditions*, 1887–9

Percy, T., *Reliques of Ancient English Poetry*, 1765, Everyman ed., 1906

Porter, E., *The Folklore of East Anglia*, 1974

Ploss, E. E., *Siegfried-Sigurd der Drachenkämpfer*, 1966

Pritchard, J. B., *Ancient Near Eastern Texts Relating to the Old Testament*, 1955

Readers' Digest Publications, *Folklore, Myths and Legends of Britain*, 1973

Rhys, Sir John, *Celtic Folk-Lore*, 1901

Risdon, T., *A Survey of Devon*, c.1630 (reprint 1970)

Robertson, R. M., *Selected Highland Folktales*, 1961 (reprint 1977)

Rudder, S., *A New History of Gloucestershire*, 1779

Rudkin, E. H., *Lincolnshire Folk-Lore*, 1936 (reprint 1973)

Sharp, Sir Cuthbert (attrib.) *The Worm of Lambton*. 1830; reprinted in *The Bishoprick Garland*, 1834

Smith, Sir Grafton E., *The Evolution of the Dragon*, 1919

Simpson, J., *The Folklore of Sussex*, 1973

Simpson, J., *The Folklore of the Welsh Border*, 1976

Stuart, G. B., 'The Dragon's Pool', *Sussex County Magazine* VI, 1932, 154–6

Stubbes, P., *The Anatomie of Abuses*, 1583

Sweeney, J. B., *A Pictorial History of Sea Monsters*, 1972

Tongue, R., 'Billy Biter and the Parkin', *Folklore* LXXVIII, 1969, 139–41

Tongue, R., *Somerset Folklore*, 1965

Topsell, E., *The History of Serpents*, 1608

Trevelyan, M., *Folk-Lore and Folk Stories of Wales*, 1909

Whistler, C.W., 'Local Traditions in the Quantocks', *Folklore XIX*, 1908

Whitlock, Ralph, *Here Be Dragons, 1983*

*Wonderful Legend of the Lambton Worm, The*, n.d., c.1875 (reprint 1968)

Woolmer, D., 'New Light on the White Horse', *Folklore* LXXVIII, 1969, 90–112

# Index